D1554515

TOTAL

PASS

DEFENSE

Lloyd H. Helgeson

PARKER PUBLISHING COMPANY, Inc.
West Nyack, New York

© 1978 *by*

Parker Publishing Company, Inc.
West Nyack, New York

Library of Congress Cataloging in Publication Data

Helgeson, Lloyd H
   Total pass defense.

   Includes index.
    1. Passing (Football). 2. Football--Defense.
3. Football coaching. I. Title.
GV951.5.H44   796.33'22   77-24675
ISBN 0-13-925628-8

Printed in the United States of America

HOW THIS BOOK WILL HELP YOU

Total Pass Defense is an in-depth study of all aspects of pass defense. This book will help you to develop a better pass defense for your particular situation or to improve the one you are now using.

If rushing the passer has been one of your team's problems, you will find information and techniques here which have never been covered in coaching clinics or other publications. Eight different individual techniques for destroying passer protection are described. With a little practice your players can master the Judo technique—or perhaps they will favor the "club" technique. Among the eight methods of attacking an offensive blocker there are at least one or two that each of your defensive linemen can master.

The overload principle of pass rush is examined and explained. Many coaching points, individual drills, and unit drills for developing a successful pass rush are included. Stunts, red-dogs, loops and slants are discussed as methods of achieving the overload. How to assign keys and teach reaction to keys will help you take the gamble out of this aspect of pass defense and make your rushing unit more effective.

This book gives you the four objectives in delaying receivers and shows you how to teach your defensive players the necessary techniques to frustrate opposing quarterbacks and destroy the timing of their pass offenses.

Zone, man-for-man and combination coverage systems are presented in detail and evaluated. In these chapters the pros and cons of each system are discussed, personnel requirements are assessed and the many types of coverages, rotations, and adjustments from each system are illustrated and explained. New methods of teaching your players the concept of pass defense zones and the use of "zone points" and keying are offered. Special sections show you how to cover the deep zones, the short zones, the inside zones, and the outside zones.

Individual techniques of every popular coverage are presented—from stance and footwork to stripping and intercepting. Whether you use a three-deep zone, a four-deep man-for-man, or combination defense, many valuable points in these chapters will help improve your pass defense.

Do you have trouble coping with an opponent that has an outstanding receiver? This book illustrates a variety of double coverages from each system and shows you how to disguise these defenses, increase your interception rate, and force your opponent to throw to less capable secondary receivers.

Perhaps you are having trouble with your undercoverage. How many times have your opponents completed a short pass on third down to keep their drive alive? Of special interest, then, will be the sections dealing with the linebackers in pass defense. Since their responsibilities and techniques are so vastly different from the deep backs, they are given special attention in each system.

You will find that even the special problems of weather and field conditions, play-action and sprint-out passes, and goal line and prevent defenses are given an extensive treatment (Chapter 11).

This book is not a presentation of a single pass defense system, it is a coach's text on pass defense, presenting concepts and techniques gleaned from 25 years of experience on the high school, junior college, college, and university levels. It is a comprehensive book that will stimulate you to re-examine your own pass defense and it will be a source of valuable coaching points that are certain to improve your pass defense!

Lloyd H. Helgeson

Contents

Chapter 1

DEVELOPING THE
TOTAL PASS DEFENSE

PASS DEFENSE—THE NEGLECTED PHASE OF FOOTBALL

Pass defense has been traditionally one of the most neglected aspects of high school and college football. Probably less practice time is allocated to pass defense in the average team's weekly practice schedule than to any other major phase of the game. If your opponent is spending half of his offensive practice periods concentrating on his pass offense, which constitutes 50 percent of his total offense (the goal of "balance" which most pass-minded coaches strive for), then it is certainly advisable that half of the defensive time allocated to preparing for that opponent should be devoted to pass defense.

This phase of the game has to be sold not only to the coaching staff but also to the players. Most boys like to throw the ball or run out for passes and as they report daily on the practice field they will participate naturally in these activities. But seldom will an individual player be seen in this pre-practice period working on his stance, balance, footwork, and the movements essential to good pass defense. If you are to field a sound defensive team, you will have to interest your players in this phase of the game and develop individual, unit, and team pride in the pass defense.

There is a psychological advantage to the team that can present a strong overall defense. Most offensive minded teams evidence strain when confronted by a strong defense that consistently denies them the quick thrust or the long drive for a touchdown. Repeated frustration of the offensive team by good defensive plays builds up a tenseness on the part of the offensive players, who may compound their problems with faulty ball handling, errors in assignments, and unnecessary penalties. Unless the team is superbly conditioned and disciplined, these conditions can lead to the deterioration of their team spirit, morale, and unity.

These results should be spelled out as desirable objectives of the defensive team and should be borne in mind by each defensive player during the game. Each tackle, each pass that is knocked down or intercepted, every offensive drive that is stopped not only gains the football for your own offensive team, but also contributes to the build-up of tension and anxiety on the part of the opponent's offense, making it less and less effective.

ESTABLISHING A DEFENSE

The foundation of a good defense is the philosophy upon which it is built, and the philosophy of the pass defense cannot be divorced from the philosophy of the total defense. The two must be interwoven and mutually support each other.

A coach and his staff must first establish a clear-cut defensive philosophy for their team. This is the anchor for all of their defensive thinking. Agreement on a single philosophy assures staff coordination and united effort in the planning and drilling and coaching that go into the molding of a team's total defensive effort. The principles established to initiate that philosophy become the guidelines that your defensive captain and signal caller rely upon to intelligently direct the defense under game conditions.

Most defensive philosophies relate to only two basic concepts: (1) containment, and (2) penetration.

Are your intentions to merely "contain" the offensive team, holding each gain to minimum yardage, avoiding the quick touchdown, the long pass or run, and hoping that the offensive team will eventually make an error that will destroy their drive? This is what some coaches refer to as the "rubber-band philosophy"—stretch but don't break.

Or do you believe in penetration—the offensive defense——attacking the opponent, forcing his mistakes, and maintaining maximum pressure on the offensive team?

Maybe you like a combination of these two philosophies, changing and varying as to the game situation. It is very effective, but difficult to teach to inexperienced players. The penetration techniques call for extreme aggressiveness and physical power, whereas the containment techniques require a softer touch, immediate reaction, and great pursuit. The development of the capacity to effect this change of pace requires considerable team and individual discipline and many hours of arduous drill and hard work.

But whatever overall defensive philosophy you select, it must also be compatible with your *offensive* philosophy. The offense and defense must complement each other. One must assist the other in the overall game plan. If your offense is a typical pro-spread, drop-back offense featuring a 50-50 pass-run ratio and hoping for a fair share of home run passes, then the defense should be a fierce, aggressive, penetrating type which will get the ball back as often and as quickly as possible.

The wide open type of offense, heavy on passing, will turn over the ball more frequently than most offenses and consequently needs strong defensive support. In the average high school game, for example, a team will obtain possession of the ball approximately 15 times. A pass completion rate of 50 percent is very good, but even at this rate, a passing team that is not built on a ball control pass offense philosophy will frequently be inconsistent and, as a result, not get its normal share of plays from each period of possession. If, in turn, this team is playing a containment type defense against an opponent's ball control offense, neither will they gain possession of the ball the normal number of times during the game.

A pass-minded coach must accept the fact that there will be those days when his quarterback cannot "hit the ocean with a mop." If the game develops into a pattern of three incomplete passes and a punt, the defensive philosophy had better be one of aggression to regain the ball as quickly as possible so the law of averages can assist the erratic passer!

So defensive philosophy must be related to offensive philosophy. Neither can stand independently in a well organized football program. Each of these philosophies should be established as soon as an evaluation of the elements of the coming season can be made. Qualifications of the coaching staff, skills of available player personnel, and the nature of the teams on the schedule are considerations one must weigh in developing a philosophy.

When completed, the offensive and defensive philosophies should be published and distributed to all members of the staff and all the players. They should be supplemented with specific principles which will implement the philosophies expressed. These principles should, provide positive guidelines to the staff and team leaders.

DEFENSIVE PHILOSOPHY AND PRINCIPLES

Philosophy

In modern football a prime requisite of a good football team is a sound defense. The schools that consistently win are those whose coaches and players are well schooled in the fundamental techniques of individual defense.

Our philosophy of defensive football is based upon a desire to *hold every gain to a minimum* and *get the ball back as quickly as possible*. We want the ball in the hands of our offensive team—and we would like to gain possession of it as close to our opponent's goal line as possible.

We are an offensive-minded team, which implies that the majority of our practice time will be devoted to offense. As a consequence, we require a sound defensive system which can be learned with a minimum of practice time. Our defenses must be simple, yet capable of meeting the current variety of offenses with a minimum number of adjustments.

Our emphasis is on establishing a fundamental approach to defensive football, breaking down teaching methods, establishing each player's responsibilities, and being sure that each player can perform his assignments. We believe in establishing a few basic alignments with a few basic adjustments as opposed to a large number of defenses which complicate adjustments to various offenses and offensive "sets."

Consequently, we believe in the use of only two basic defensive formations in the overall plan of defense. We have adjustment rules from these defenses to suit unusual formations such as spreads, split ends, etc. In both of our basic defenses our linemen play a control-charge type of defense with pre-determined keys and reactions for any type of blocking pattern they might meet. In addition, we use "red-dogging." We use this technique from 15 percent to 25 percent of the time and play our normal keying defenses the remainder of the time.

Our emphasis on offense does not mean that we minimize the importance of defense. In fact defense is *vital* to our offense. We do not normally play ball control football, consequently we may give up the ball more frequently than ball control teams. This means that our defense must be adept at regaining possession for us. It means that our defense must "carry the game to our opponent." We must be the aggressor, punish the opponent for every yard that he gains, and force him to make mistakes.

Principles

A. Keep the game *inside of* us and *in front* of us.

1. *Force the offense.*

We want our defense to play an "offensive defense"—always ready to take advantage of an offensive team's mistakes and, through an all-out sustained effort in team play, to force an offensive team to make mistakes that can provide defensive scores or offensive scores by turning the ball over to the offense in a favorable position on the field. Our line and linebackers are our forcers.

2. *Contain the Offense.*

We want to confine the offense to a small area of the playing field. There must be defense in width to cover the field laterally, and there must be defense in depth so that if one line of defenders fails to stop the play, another will be in position to do so. Our ends, outside linebackers, and halfbacks are the containers.

3. *Pursue and gang tackle.*

Each player has secondary responsibilities as well as his primary responsibility. Pursuit and gang tackling are secondary responsibilities of every man on the defensive team.

B. Change, conceal, and shift defenses.

1. *Change defenses.*

Our purpose in changing defenses is to create uncertainty for the offensive quarterbacks as to what defense to expect. Each defense presents different problems for the offense and where there are weaknesses in each defense due to alignment and personnel, we do not want the offensive team to be able to know just what defensive weakness will be present. The more successful a defense is on a given day, the less likely we are to change defenses often. We will naturally want to stick with the defenses which are doing the best job of stopping our opponents.

2. *Conceal defenses.*

We conceal our defenses so as to mislead the offensive team as to our defensive weaknesses. We present an alignment which appears to be different from what we actually end up in when the ball is snapped. We want to lure the offense into attacking what appears to be a weakness, but in reality is a strength of our defense.

3. *Shift defenses.*

We shift our defenses to present problems to the offensive blockers and the quarterback. Our shifting takes place after the offensive team has lined up on the ball. We initially present an alignment that is different from the alignment we will be in when the ball is snapped. The offensive blockers must adjust their assignments from one defense to another in a relatively short space of time. We hope to cause confusion and a lack of poise and assurance for the offense.

C. Defend opponent's strengths.

We want to use our best defenses against their strength to stop the offensive maneuvers in which they have confidence and which have been successful for them. We want to meet strength with strength and force them to change their offensive tactics to do things they are not accustomed to doing. We feel they will not do them as well as their normal "bread and butter" plays.

D. Have a defensive "game plan."

The defensive game plan will be based upon the knowledge of our opponent gained from scouting reports and analysis of his game films. This will be a simple plan for the employment of our defenses in this particular game and will include appropriate adjustments and keys to meet our opponent's strengths.

E. **Be fundamentally sound in individual defensive techniques.**

While we feel there are many things that can contribute to a successful team defense, by far the most important is for all eleven defensive players to be fundamentally sound in the techniques of their individual positions. No matter what our defensive alignment or philosophy, a defense will not be any stronger than the individuals who make it up. Each player must constantly strive to improve his individual techniques in all things he is required to do on defense. He must constantly practice and strive for perfection in all techniques he must perform.

ESTABLISHING A PHILOSOPHY OF PASS DEFENSE

Having determined a guiding philosophy for defense in general, one should next consider a philosophy of pass defense. What will be your approach to this phase of the game next season? Where will your emphasis lie? What kind of material do you have and what are they capable of doing with respect to pass defense?

Most coaches will agree that there are three aspects of pass defense: (1) rushing the passer, (2) holding up or delaying receivers, and (3) covering the pass after it is thrown. Any pass defense philosophy then must be specific as to these aspects. Where will you place your emphasis? Ideally, of course, one would like to be proficient in all phases of defense, but unfortunately our material and the capabilities of our opponents make it advisable to concentrate on those things which we feel we can do best. Against a good sound passing team it is almost impossible on any given play to rush, delay, and cover with equal strength and intensity. A linebacker charged with a pass defense responsibility can give only token assistance in delaying receivers and obviously cannot participate in the pass rush. The team effort on a specific play must be of necessity weighted toward the accomplishment of but one or two of the three aspects of pass defense. If a team balances its strength in an effort to do all these on every play, chances are that nothing will be accomplished successfully. The same can be said for an entire season. If the coaching staff fails to analyze its personnel's strengths and weaknesses and consequently never determines the team's potentials in pass defense, that team may flounder from game to game, never developing its true capacities, trying to cover everything and being efficient in nothing.

It is a responsibility of the coaching staff to determine the team's potentials and then to develop them. A small, light, inexperienced defensive line will probably never become adequate in pressuring the drop-back passer. A defensive backfield which lacks speed will be hard pressed to provide adequate coverage. But every team will have a potential in one or two of these pass defense aspects—it is the staff's responsibility to identify that strength, develop it and incorporate it into a philosophy which will guide that team throughout the season.

The following is a pass defense philosophy developed by the author and his staff for a recent season:

The most effective pass defense system is one that coordinates the three basic methods of pass defense: rushing the passer, delaying receivers, and covering the pass. It is not advisable to use exclusively any one of the above methods of defending against passes. From scouting reports, the tendencies of an opponent in regard to down, distance, field position, etc. can be determined and the type defense called which will best counteract what they like to do in various situations.

Basically, we will cover all zones effectively, but on long yardage situations and as a change of pace we will rush with seven or eight men. On crucial passing situations we will jam or delay the opponent's favorite receiver.

The primary objective of our pass defense is to prevent the completion of the long pass but all completed passes must be held to a low total net yardage. Our second objective is to get the football.

Our pass defense system will be developed with a minimum of change in basic defensive patterns and techniques. Simplicity will characterize the defense: however, this simplicity will be disguised by using different alignments, frequently changing alignments, rotating, and adjusting so the offensive quarterback cannot anticipate the defense in any given situation. We hope to minimize the effectiveness of our opponent's passing attack by varying our coverage and using the different methods of pass defense.

COACHING DEFENSE

It's not what you know, it's what you can teach that wins football games. Coaching is teaching and the secret of success in teaching is good organization. We all know fellow coaches who are knowledgeable and experienced in their field, but nevertheless prove to be ineffective. Quite frequently these gentlemen were outstanding performers themselves and yet their teams reflect very little of the expertise of their mentors. On the other hand, we also know members of our profession who win, and win, and win, regardless of the different coaching environments in which they are placed. Whenever I talk to one of these coaches or visit their practice sessions or hear their presentations at coaching clinics, I am always impressed by the organization and attention to details that they evidence.

The same principles that make a classroom teacher effective make an athletic coach effective. The difference, however, is that the classroom professor can deliver his lecture and walk out. His attitude can be "take it or leave it." He may flunk half the class and everyone is awe-stricken. The coach, however, has to be a super-teacher, if he flunks half the class, he flunks with them.

To teach is to communicate and one of the first essentials of communication is a common language. I have found it very helpful from time to time to sit down with my staff and compile a list of all of the football terminology that we commonly use. My intention is to attain a standardization of our football language to avoid confusion and misunderstanding on the part of our players. This list of terms and their definitions becomes a part of the player handbooks of all squads in our system and each coaching staff (freshman, junior varsity, varsity) devotes a large part of its first classroom squad meeting to a presentation and discussion of this terminology.

Many coaches fail to appreciate the advantages of the classroom as a part of their instructional program. So frequently I view football practice sessions in which the coaching staff has broken the squad into appropriate groups for unit work, but no one is working! In the middle of each group an assistant coach is talking while ten or fifteen players listen half-heartedly, arms folded, shifting their weight from one foot to the other. The classroom is the place to talk. When a team moves onto the practice field, it should be for the purpose of accomplishing those things that cannot be done in the classroom. Nothing can disrupt a spirited practice session more than a long-winded dissertation by one of the coaches. Field time is valuable and should be reserved for activity—developing skills, learning technique, and correcting errors. Don't waste it on instruction which can be accomplished somewhere else.

The desirable sequence of most instruction is in four parts: (1) presentation, (2) demonstration, (3) application, and (4) evaluation. A great deal of step number one can be accomplished in the classroom, whether one is coaching football or springboard diving. Here is the place to present the theory of your defense to the team—to give them the "big picture." I have found it is a good practice to prepare this presentation well in advance and to put all diagrams on overhead projection transparencies to eliminate diagramming on a blackboard, consequently speeding up the presentation.

Present the defense in its simplest form first. Illustrate it against a balanced line, balanced backfield formation such as the full house T, then, only after it is fully understood under these circumstances, indicate the adjustments to split ends, flankers, slot-backs, and the variety of other offensive alignments you may anticipate defending.

As you go over the defenses, indicating the positions of each player, also outline his responsibilities, stance, charge, and movement and reactions on the snap of the ball. This should be done briefly at this time and each player provided with a mimeographed summary sheet of his position to be inserted in his player's handbook. As an example, the following is a summary sheet which I have provided for middle guard candidates in presenting our Oklahoma or "50" defense:

MIDDLE GUARD

A. *Position*

    1.   Depth will vary with the tactical situation and your ability to move with the ball

    2.   Usually from two to three feet from the ball

        a.   In short-yardage situations play closer

        b.   In long-yardage situations play more loosely

    3.   Square up with the center

B. *Responsibilities*

   1. Responsible for running plays to either side of center

   2. Responsible for the draw play and center screen

   3. Responsible to rush the passer

   4. Responsible for the quarterback sneak

C. *Stance*

   1. Toe to instep

   2. Legs well up under you

   3. Be squared away with the center

      a. Able to take a short step in either direction quickly

      b. Able to play pressure from either side

D. *Charge*

   1. Eyes on the center—peripheral vision to movement of the guards.

   2. Short steps—avoid a long initial step

   3. Deliver a blow

      a. Two-hand shiver

      b. Strike an upward blow with heels of hands to opponent's shoulders

      c. Lock wrists and elbows and drive until you release to the ball

E. *Movement*

   1. As soon as you determine the way in which the center is trying to take you, quickly *fight around the head* of the blocker

   2. Feet up under the body

   3. Fight pressure from the guards

      a. Re-direct charge through the guard

      b. Do not allow yourself to be moved laterally

      c. Drive through resistance

      d. A collapse of the middle guard when double pressure is placed upon him will cause collapse of the entire defense

   4. Pursue parallel to the line of scrimmage—do not overrun the ball carrier

At the conclusion of the presentation session, every member of the team will have a general idea of the nature and responsibilities of all positions. The mutual support and coordination that the defense requires should be fully understood and all members should understand how all the pieces fit together. Too frequently, coaches overlook the values of presenting this overall view of the total team effort and jump right into coaching individual technique on the field. The inevitable result is that the players fail to appreciate the significance of their assignments and never fully develop the fine teamwork so essential to good defense. When the unexpected happens, a strange offensive alignment or an unanticipated play series, such teams are incapable of making intelligent adjustments on their own and, as a result, confusion sets in and confidence ebbs.

DEVELOP INDIVIDUAL TECHNIQUE

I have discussed defensive football with a number of coaches who admit to minimizing the development of individual technique in their defensive preparations. Their concentration seems to be on the use of multiple defenses, a maximum of jumping and stunting, and the development of an aggressive attitude. This method of team defense leans heavily on the creation of confusion on the part of the offensive team. It is not difficult to devise a defensive system in which by slight adjustment of individual positions one can present as many as 20 or 30 different alignments to the offense during a single game. The hope and intention is to create errors in blocking assignments, destroy the quarterback's ability to call appropriate plays, and to disrupt the offensive timing and finesse.

To me this is Russian roulette on the football field and it develops into a guessing game between the offensive and defensive signal callers. Good defense should imply stability, consistency, and dependability, and these qualities cannot be developed without a heavy emphasis on the development of individual technique. Good offensive teams will not be confused by a variety of defenses and a smart quarterback can manipulate the multiple defense team into desirable alignments by utilizing various offensive sets.

A limited number of team defenses which, in turn, affords ample practice time to develop the techniques of each position in each defense to the optimum seems to be a more sound approach. To initiate this system the coaching staff must first analyze each position of each defense, breaking each defender's actions into fundamental skills that will enable him to perform his assignments with maximum efficiency. For example, let us look at the middle guard position previously referred to in this chapter. The first skill requirement of this position is to assume a proper stance, and having accomplished this, the candidate must next master the head-on charge, then reaction to the movement of the center, reaction to the pressure of a double team by either guard, pass block reaction, pursuit, play against the fullback draw and center screen pass, and a host of other techniques which will be required of him. A list of skills such as this must be compiled for each position, then the staff can devise the training methods and drills that will develop these skills.

Do not waste time teaching techniques or developing skills which will not be used in a game. For years I have heard coaches talk about their interception call—a word that they teach their pass defenders to yell when they are about to intercept a pass. To alert their teammates so they can immediately pick up blocks to support the interception run-back, teams are instructed to shout "Oskie," "Geronimo," "Wahoo," or a variety of other key words—but to this day I have never heard an interceptor yell anything during a game, he is too intent on playing the ball and concentrating on gaining possession to worry about key words! So why waste practice time teaching them.

Analyze the drills that you use. Do they accomplish their intended objectives? Are they efficient? A good drill is simple, easy to set up, uses a minimum of equipment, and as few players as possible who are not actually being trained for their positions in the drill. Finally, a good drill should simulate game conditions as much as possible.

Chapter 2

DEVELOPING THE
PASS DEFENSE SYSTEM

Most coaches have had too many experiences of holding an opponent's running game for two downs only to have a well-executed pass completion continue the offensive march or score a quick touchdown. As a result, more and more coaching staffs on all levels of competition are re-examining their pass defense systems, particularly with respect to the increased use of the forward pass.

Frequently, a team's pass defense system has evolved like Topsy—it just grew. It may be made of bits and pieces pasted together by a variety of staff members over a period of years, but with no real organization or continuity. In many cases, a head coach merely installs the pass defense he knew as a player or one that he adopted from a former coach whom he assisted. Actually, most things we do in coaching—drills, techniques, plays—are plagiarisms, and we frequently incorporate them into our systems without really analyzing their true worth to our own situations. Coaches are great imitators, and when a particular style of offense or defense is successful and gains considerable publicity, the next season will see duplications throughout the country—but generally less successfully applied. A recent trend to the wishbone offense and the triple-option play is a case in point. The virtues of these offensive innovations were extolled at every coaching clinic and in every coaching magazine. They had produced national champions and many Bowl winners, and across the country their intricacies were diagrammed in playbooks of hundreds of teams whose coaching staffs were eager to sample this panacea for victory. But then someone noticed that a lot of last place teams were also running from the wishbone! Careful analysis shows that some unique personnel requirements are essential to move the wishbone just as there are specific talents necessary to run any other offense successfully.

There are very few aspects of the game of football that are universally adaptable. Almost every phase must be examined with reference to the material one has available. This fact applies to pass defense as much as it does to offensive alignment, play sequences, punt formation or any other part of the game. It may be that in the selection of the pass coverage system the consideration of personnel available is more important than in any other phase—after all, inadequacy in this department can result in opponents' touchdowns faster than anything.

But the fact remains that many coaches seldom change their secondary coverage. I have heard prominent coaches say that while there have been many changes in football, the one thing that has remained the same since the late twenties is the Tennessee zone pass defense, and many coaches are still using it. Forms of the zone are the most popular of defenses today, but it doesn't take much investigation to note that the modern zones have very little in common with General Nyland's products of the 1920's. Like everything else in football, pass defenses are undergoing constant change and the successful coach must keep abreast of recent developments, constantly adjusting and modifying his own system as offenses and his own personnel change. What was successful last season may not be effective next season.

THE BASIC COVERAGE

In the establishment of a pass defense or in the re-evaluation of one's pass defense a starting point should be a review of the basic coverages. Since all pass defenses are variations of either a zone or a man-for-man, a review of the advantages and disadvantages of each is appropriate.

Zone Defense—Advantages:

1. *Requires less talented personnel.*

Obviously, speed and reaction capacity will make a good zone with relatively mediocre material. This cannot be said for the man-for-man defense wherein over-all speed is essential.

2. *Greater interception possibilities.*

Since all zone pass defenders are watching and reacting to the ball, it is only natural that more defenders will be in the vicinity of the passer's target when the ball arrives, consequently tipped or batted balls have a greater chance of falling into defenders' hands. It's like the zone in basketball—the rebounders are always in position.

3. *Greater insurance against the long touchdown pass.*

The zone defender's cardinal rule is to not let a receiver get behind him. Since he can play the receivers more loosely and still be effective, it is more difficult for a receiver to get behind him.

4. *Longer returns from interceptions.*

Again, since all defenders react toward the ball when it is thrown, an interceptor should have a number of his teammates in the general vicinity to pick up the blocks as soon as the interception is made.

5. *The run after completed passes should be held to a minimum.*

Defenders reacting toward the ball should be in position to make an immediate tackle if the pass is completed.

6. *Easier to teach than man-for-man.*

The number of techniques and maneuvers that must be taught for adequate zone coverage are quite limited for each position.

7. *Easy to make adjustments to all formations.*

Since personnel are assigned to zones it is a relatively simple procedure to adjust to offensive formations by the reassignment of zones.

8. *Nullifies the effectiveness of the receiver with outstanding "moves."*

The zone defender is less likely to be affected by the fakes, the weaving, and the cuts of the expert receiver because he is primarily watching and reacting to the ball while playing the receiver loosely in his zone.

9. Cannot run picks and screens against a zone.

Zone Defense—Disadvantages:

1. *Vulnerable to passes thrown in the seams between the zones.*

The most difficult area for the zone defender to cover is the lateral extremities of his zone, so a weakness in coverage will exist where two adjacent zones come together.

2. *Vulnerable to passes in the middle range.*

Difficult to cover passes thrown just over the linebacker areas and into the front of secondary receivers' zones.

3. *Vulnerable to flooding.*

Possible to overload two or three receivers into one zone covered by only one defender.

4. *Affords buck-passing.*

When completions are made, it is sometimes difficult to fix the responsibility, particularly if a number of receivers were downfield.

5. *Difficult to cover all zones.*

Because of the number of pass zones, it is generally necessary to leave one or two zones uncovered to provide adequate defense against the running game.

6. *Vulnerable to ball control offense.*

A good passer throwing short and medium passes into the seams can control the ball. Hooks, curls, and sidelines are especially effective.

Man-for-man Defense—Advantages:

1. *Has definite responsibilities for individual defenders.*

Since each man is assigned to an offensive receiver, there can be no excuses or buck-passing when completions are made. Assignments are clear-cut and specific.

2. *Develops the competitive urge of the individual to dominate his opponent.*

Besides the competitive team play in which the defender is involved, he is also stimulated by the personal contest between his assigned receiver and himself.

3. *Affords the matching of defensive personnel with appropriate offensive personnel.*

The most capable defender can be assigned to cover the most capable receiver thereby avoiding mis-matches.

4. *Toughest defense to throw against.*

Providing the personnel are capable, the man-for-man need not give away anything to the offense. Coverage of all areas and all patterns is possible—if the defenders are capable.

5. *Readily adjustable to all offensive "sets."*

There should be no confusion created by a variety of offensive formations since the defender need only take a position in which he can cover his assigned receiver.

6. *Affords double coverage when an assigned receiver does not get into the pattern.*

The free defender can assist adjacent defenders in double coverages where needed.

7. *It is possible to get more men rushing the passer without jeopardizing the coverage.*

Since there are but five possible receivers, six players can always be in the rush. In the zone, there are seven zones, which means that if all are to be covered only four men are left to rush.

8. *No defenders are wasted in an area where there are no receivers.*

Each man in the coverage has a man assignment; if the receiver doesn't release, the defender has a secondary responsibility.

9. *Keying an individual prevents being fooled by play action passes.*

As the key releases into the secondary, the defender is concentrating on the receiver, knows that covering him is his primary responsibility, and will be less susceptible to ball handling fakes in the offensive backfield.

Man-for-man Defense—Disadvantages:

1. *Requires above average backfield speed.*

Speed and agility are prime essentials in the man-for-man. Receivers must be covered tightly and the defenders are generally in one-on-one situations.

2. *Lack of assistance from adjacent defenders in interceptions and run-backs.*

Adjacent defenders are covering their own assigned receivers and not necessarily watching the ball, so there is less concentration of defenders in the target area where the ball is thrown.

3. *Produces more pass interference penalties.*

The individual aggressiveness and the tight coverage required of the man-for-man tends to generate more pass interference calls.

4. *Susceptible to the tackle eligible play.*

From the defensive secondary it is difficult to distinguish slight adjustments of depth by offensive players which make some players eligible and others ineligible, particularly in spread formations. A man coverage defender may in error cover an ineligible receiver, leaving an eligible man open. The tackle eligible is illegal in the pro leagues where man coverage is most popular.

5. *Slower reaction of off-side backs into rotation to run.*

Since these backs are playing men, not the ball, they may stay with their man too long to be effective in the rotation plan.

Many basic defenses are design combinations of the man-for-man and the zone. The ideal pass coverage would be provided by a unit which could give man-for-man in appropriate situations, then switch to a zone, and further confuse the opposition with a combination of these two. The defensive trend for the past several years has been away from a single type of coverage. College and high school teams that have been predominately zone-defense-oriented are rapidly incorporating the man defense into their systems, while pro teams which have used predominately man coverages are increasingly using more zone. Those coaching staffs which emphasize their pass defense and attempt to develop it fully are using three coverages: man, zone, and combination.

Combination Defense—Advantages:

1. *Can best utilize a few exceptional defenders who must be teamed with some average defenders in the unit.*

A frequent combination is to zone with linebackers who are weaker on pass defense and cover the primary receivers with man coverage by the exceptional defenders.

2. *Possible to "hide" a particularly weak pass defender.*

One man's effectiveness against the running game may demand that he be on the defensive unit. By zoning this man, his pass defense responsibility can be minimized, while the remainder of the defense plays man.

3. *Excellent to cover an outstanding receiver.*

By the combination double coverage of zoning the man in the short area and picking him up deep with man-for-man, an outstanding receiver can be double-covered effectively without complete commitment of both defenders.

4. *Allows the disguise and change-ups needed to stop various types of pass offense.*

The combination, when utilized with one or both of the other types of coverage, can be confusing to the offensive quarterback, making intelligent play selection a difficult task.

Combination—Disadvantages:

1. *Increases the amount of coaching time allocated for pass defense.*

Both man-for-man and zone techniques must be developed in the majority of defenders.

2. *Difficult to adjust to all formations:*

Offensive sets may force the combination into undesirable alignments. The combination is best utilized against specific scouted offensive sets of a particular opponent.

EVALUATION OF PERSONNEL

Besides weighing the advantages and disadvantages of coverages, many other factors must enter into your selection of coverage. For example, the pass offense styles of one's opponents should be considered. What are their potentials for next season? What is the variety of offensive formations that your team will face next season? What is the calibre of your opponent's quarterbacks? Receivers? Do your opposing coaches press the passing game with imaginative plays, precision passing, well executed patterns, or are they predominately running teams with stereotyped pass offenses? What will be their pass-run ratio? What kind of personnel do they have? And of course one of your prime considerations will be your own personnel. One should never force a pre-determined defense on a team. A good coach is flexible, capable of modifying his offense and defense to take advantage of the abilities of his team personnel.

An evaluation of one's personnel can begin with a review of game films of the previous season, and at the same time the coach can examine the effectiveness of previous team coverages used. Every pass pattern run against your team during the season should be charted. One of the simplest methods is to diagram each pass pattern on 5″ x 7″ cards indicating the defensive coverage and the personnel at each position. Indicate the field position of the ball, the down and distance, and diagram the routes of all receivers and the movements of each pass defender. At the bottom of each card indicate whether the pass was complete, incomplete, or intercepted. If it was completed or intercepted, indicate the length of the subsequent run. Finally, determine why the pass coverage was successful or unsuccessful. When, where, and how did the coverage break down? Were the completions the result of individual error or the system itself?

Having charted this information on separate cards for each play, it is now a simple procedure to evaluate for specific personnel, situations, formations, or whatever else may be of value to your future planning. If you are analyzing your sophomore corner linebacker, for example, check all cards to determine if he was in proper position for the coverage called, then separate those cards in which his assigned receiver was the intended receiver. How successful was he in the coverage. What error did he consistently make? Was he beaten by the commission of mental errors or physical errors? Is he more effective in one particular style of defensive play than another?

Such a detailed analysis of filmed pass coverage produces many implications, not only for the better utilization of personnel, but for better team defense as well. By separating the cards in which you were in zone, man-for-man, or a particular adjustment or rotation, one can very easily evaluate the effectiveness of these team coverages.

CONSTRUCTING A DEFENSE

We are all aware that on defense nothing can beat a team faster than the long pass—a basic defensive axiom is *prevent the long gainer*. With this factor in mind it follows that the construction of any defense should start with the placement of the defensive backs.

Whether to be three deep or four deep is an early decision that must be made. Most man-for-man teams play out of a four-deep alignment while most zone teams function from either the three-deep or four-deep alignments. A recent innovation in the combination defenses is to play close man-for-man on the tight end and split receivers while backing them up deep with a two-man zone. The availability of qualified backs to play the deep positions will be the most important factor in determining the number of defenders in the deep coverage. It would be foolish to start building a four-deep man-for-man if only two players with above average speed were available.

Next, determine a containment plan for outside running plays. We tend to think of the line and linebackers as being responsible for runs and the defensive backs as responsible for passes, however, these are really only priorities. One must think of the whole—all eleven players have a responsibility for both pass and run. Pass defense starts with an aggressive line and works back to the safety man—good run defense starts with strong secondary support in the containment plan. Interior linemen and linebackers can do a better job of plugging the opponent's inside running game when they have confidence that the outside attack will be properly

sealed. All personnel must be placed with respect to both responsibilities, pass and run, for against good competition neither can be
sacrificed.

The defensive backs must have clear-cut assignments for
carrying out their responsibilities to stop the outside running
game. In the total defensive scheme someone must be assigned the
containment responsibility, someone must have the off-tackle area
and someone must have the "fill" responsibility.

A number of years ago a philosophy of "run 'em into the
sideline" was popular in defensing the outside game. However, it
has recently fallen into disrepute because of the number of offensive backs who were able to "beat 'em to the sideline" and turn
upfield for long gains. This technique is still employed as a
change-up by many coaches and is valuable also against certain
types of alignments and specific plays, but most coaches now like to
fix the outside running responsibility to one man. He is the defender who is expected to draw a line in front of the runner moving
laterally and say, "Thou shalt not pass!" He determines the lateral
boundary of the defensive team's perimeter on his side of the field,
and his job is to stop the runner at that point or force him to cut
inside. He is not to be confused with the "contain" man in the pass
rush, the man who is charged with keeping the quarterback in a
specific area. They may be one and the same occasionally, but
frequently the outside containers against rushing plays has a pass
responsibility to which he moves on key when a pass shows.

If the contain man does his job properly, then the runner
will be forced to cut in to the man with off-tackle responsibility
pursuing on an inside-out route. If the onside inside linebacker has
been able to get into his pursuit pattern, he too will be putting a
pincer movement on the runner from the inside, while the contain
man continues pressure from the outside-in. The intention of
course is to trap the ball carrier in this pinch or at least to restrict
him to as narrow a running lane as possible as he approaches the
line of scrimmage. Next the defensive backs play their vital role in
the ground defense. Diagram 2-1 illustrates one method of this
secondary support from a wide tackle six and an Oklahoma 5-4-2.

Having read a "run" key, the outside back and his adjacent
inside back come up on converging routes to meet the ball carrier
as close as they can to the line of scrimmage. The outside back is
supporting the contain man; he is coming up from an outside angle
intending to meet the ball carrier just inside the contain man, but

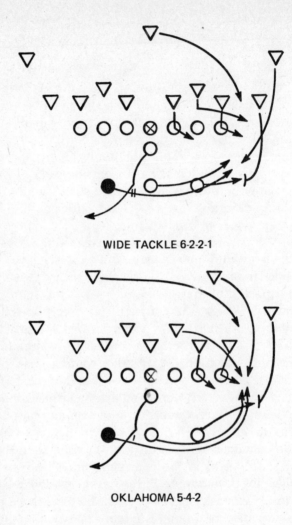

WIDE TACKLE 6-2-2-1

OKLAHOMA 5-4-2

Diagram 2-1

he must be wary of a quick outside cut by the ball carrier so he concentrates on tackling with the inside shoulder. The adjacent inside back is coming up on a slight inside-out angle and he is conscious of cuts to his inside, so he concentrates on tackling with his outside shoulder. If both of these backs have been well prepared for their opponent, provided with positive keys, and react with confidence and aggressiveness, they can stymie an opponent's outside attack. Frequently, the contain man and one of the inside

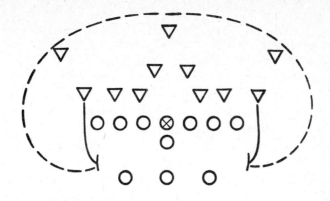

Diagram 2-2

pursuers will be in the process of tackling the runner just as these two backs arrive at full speed at the line of scrimmage. In that case their job is to "level" off the pile," a tactic which discourages outside runners.

Many coaches overlook the requirement for a containment plan when they adjust their defenses for certain situations. Sometimes stunting patterns put the contain man on an inside route with no one picking up his outside responsibility. Faulty rotation plans can also disrupt the containment as well as poorly conceived plans to meet the option plays and sprint-outs.

The defensive backfield needs definite responsibilities for the support of the running defense in all circumstances. Knowing exactly what their running responsibilities are makes for better pass defense. The backs can be positive in their reactions and will move more quickly into their assignments, regardless of whether the developing play is a pass or run.

Having placed the deep backs and contain men, a defensive perimeter will have been established around the offensive team. (Diagram 2-2). The objective now, of course, is to keep the football inside this perimeter, which in turn assures that no cheap touchdowns will be scored from long gainers. From this point the defensive alignment can be completed by a variety of arrangements of the interior linemen and linebackers.

But just as it is necessary to constantly change the alignment at the line of scrimmage to disrupt the running game, it is also necessary to constantly change the backfield alignment to disrupt the pass offense. Every team defense has its weaknesses, and likewise, there is no perfect pass defense. A good quarterback will eventually destroy a single alignment or a single type of coverage. If the opposition can consistently predict your defense, he has the advantage of being able to always strike your vulnerable areas.

Confusion at the line of scrimmage can be created by alternating two or three basic arrangements of the line and linebackers, by stunts, red-dogging, jumping defenses, and a variety of other techniques. Similar strategies must be employed in the defensive backfield to destroy the quarterback's capacity for intelligent pass play selection in the huddle, forcing him to resort to the use of automatics, a hazardous device at best. A number of these techniques for varying or disguising the pass defense coverage will be discussed in later chapters, but a word of caution about their use—don't have too many. Giving a team too many defenses, too many variations, and too many techniques can lead to confusion, indecision, and a reduction in the reaction time which is so vital to good defense. Good defensive play must be reflex action, its movements automatic. There isn't time for conscious thought. Like Pavlov's dog, one must be conditioned, drilled to react to a stimulus—the movement of the offensive man or the ball. If too many defenses or techniques are employed without sufficient time to master them, the defenders start thinking instead of reacting which leads to a condition I refer to as "paralysis by analysis."

Chapter 3

ESTABLISHING THE FIRST LINE OF PASS DEFENSE— RUSHING THE PASSER

Regardless of what philosophy of defense one adopts to guide the general planning for the season, when it comes to rushing the passer, the defensive concept must be to *attack*. In its usual connotation, defense means to defend something, as in the game of football, the line of scrimmage or the goal line, but this definition is too passive to be applied to pass defense. When a pass shows or the game situation indicates "pass," defensive linemen who are a part of the rushing unit must be the aggressors, prime examples of the offensive defense.

A good pass rush has several objectives, the most obvious of which is to tackle the passer. If this is not accomplished, however, the rush is still effective if it has forced the quarterback to throw a bad pass. Dumping the quarterback must actually be considered a bonus against a good passing team because it is a difficult thing to do. Consider the professional teams. As many games as they play and as many passes as they throw, the NFL defensive pass rush leaders usually dump the quarterback an average of only three times a game. To evaluate the effectiveness of one's pass rush on only this basis would be erroneous.

A good passer, if given the time to throw, will complete a very high percentage of his passes, so the rush should be considered effective if it has forced the quarterback to throw off-balance or to throw early before the receiver is open. A properly executed rush with the defenders in proper lanes and arms extended at the proper moment can obscure the passer's vision leading to an erratic pass. In addition, there is always the possibility that a charging lineman may tip the pass as it is thrown, bat the ball down, or even make an interception himself.

Another objective of a strong pass rush is to eliminate the long pass. Generally speaking, if deep passes, passes beyond 20 yards, are being completed against your team, then the pass rush is inadequate, the quarterback is being given too much time to throw and the receivers too much time to maneuver.

Don't underestimate the psychological effect of smothering a passer before he can throw. Nothing is more discouraging to a quarterback than having one or two fierce linemen ram him while he searches for his receiver. It is an unusual quarterback who, after a few good thumps, doesn't panic a bit and start throwing early. Even the best will lose some of their poise and accuracy.

TWO APPROACHES TO RUSHING

There are two significant approaches to the problem of developing an effective pass rush: (1) the overload principle, and (2) emphasis on individual technique. Probably most teams rely on the overload principle since it is the simplest means of effecting an adequate rush and requires the least amount of coaching. Most passer protection systems are designed to provide three blockers on each side of the center (Diagram 3-1), consequently the overload system is based on rushing more than three defenders on one side (Diagram 3-2). The success of this approach rests on outnumbering, overpowering, and surprising the blocker.

The second approach, emphasizing individual technique, is one of the most neglected phases of defensive line play. Its basis is to develop each defensive lineman's skill in combating the passer protection blocker to the point where, working as a unit, four, five, or six linemen can effectively rush the passer without an overload, leaving additional personnel available for coverage.

As in most aspects of football, it is impossible to say that one method is superior to the other. A good defensive package will utilize both, alternating sufficiently to keep the offensive team off balance and never allowing them to predict the pattern of the pass rush.

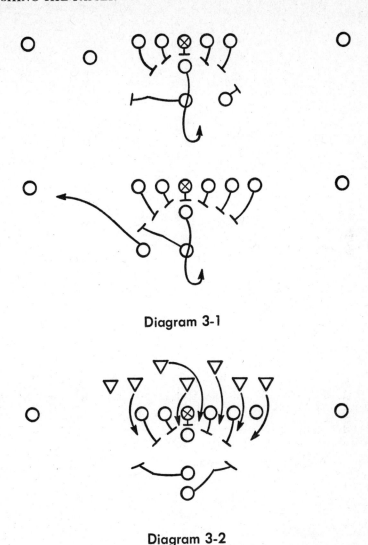

Diagram 3-1

Diagram 3-2

Regardless of which approach is emphasized, however, someone in the interior of the defensive alignment must always be assigned responsibility for draw plays, quarterback sneak, and center screen passes. These responsibilities may be divided as in an Oklahoma defense, wherein the middle guard might check the quarterback sneak while one of the linebackers covers the draw and center screens. In a pro-43 defense the tackles (guards) and middle linebacker could share these assignments. Coaches frequently overlook transferring these responsibilities when the assigned defender is on a stunt or red-dog pattern that takes him out of the area. Likewise, the rushing pattern must be coordinated with the defensive secondary to assure adequate coverage of most likely patterns and favorite receivers.

Another important principle is to vary the number of rushers and the rush pattern. Don't give up the same zones too many times in succession or a smart quarterback will soon take advantage of it. No matter how effective one pass rush may be, a change of pace is essential. This change should be not only in the rushing pattern but also in the coverage and the delay of receivers.

THE OVERLOAD

To outnumber the offensive blockers it is not necessary to rush more men than the offense has in the passer protection scheme. It is only necessary to outnumber them in a given area, thus the overload principle. The intention is to force a two-on-one situation at some point rather than rushing eight defenders against seven pass blockers, hoping that one of them, someplace, will get through.

A basic consideration of play-to-play pass defense is to determine how many players to rush and how many to cover. It is not sound football to rush less than three or more than eight. Three rushers will seldom drop the quarterback for a loss or force him to throw early, but they can confine him to the passer protection pocket and force him to throw the ball in a reasonable time. (Diagram 3-3).

The obvious advantage of the three-man rush is that it allows an eight-man coverage—every pass defense zone will be occupied. On the other hand, eight rushers can put the maximum pressure on the passer and still leave three defenders for pass coverage. It is dangerous to gamble with the three deep areas so one should never rush more than eight men.

The eight-man rush can be a balanced rush as shown in Diagram 3-4 since it naturally provides four men on each side of the center. Unless there are only two receivers in the pass pattern this charge will produce an overload on one side of the center or the other, and one of the blockers will be faced with a two-on-one situation.

An equally effective rush can be accomplished from the six- and seven-man fronts by concentrating on one area, rushing four

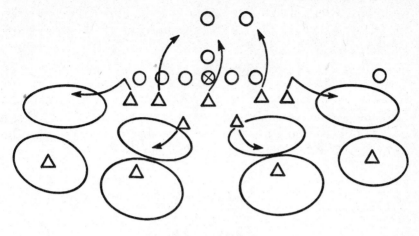

Diagram 3-3

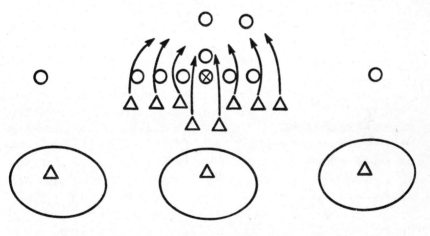

Diagram 3-4

men on one side of the center. Diagrams 3-5 through 3-8 illustrate several ways of accomplishing this. It must be emphasized to the rushers that in all of these examples some pass zones must be left uncovered, consequently they must not give the quarterback time to throw the long pass. Coverage has been sacrificed to gain rushing strength.

Overloads from five-, six-, and seven-man lines generally involve slanting or looping on the part of some linemen and the red-dogging of one or more linebackers. These movements must be disguised and accomplished with great quickness to avoid the

Diagram 3-5   **Diagram 3-6**

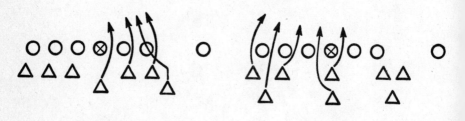

Diagram 3-7   **Diagram 3-8**

offensive blocker and to gain penetration. Prior to the snap of the ball, the defender has the advantage over his offensive opponent; he knows where he is going and in what direction he intends to charge, but if he has been schooled to react defensively only to the movement of the offensive lineman opposite him, he will be giving up this advantage. Whenever a defensive man's assignment is to charge on a predetermined path to this inside or outside he should key the snap of the football. Whenever he is on a path that sends him through a man over whom he is aligned, he keys his opponent. The same principle holds true for linebackers. Normally, linebackers should be coached to react to specific offensive players or offensive keys, but when they are on a predetermined red-dog or blitz charge, they should key the football to get a split-second jump on their offensive opponent.

    This is not to imply that stunting linemen and linebackers should not have keys, but rather that they will read their key *as they commence their charge*. Let us look at Diagram 3-9. Here the

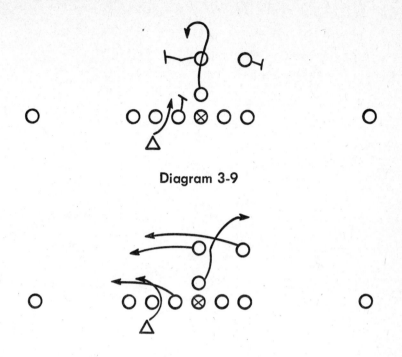

Diagram 3-9

Diagram 3-10

defensive tackle has looped to his inside and is directing a charge which, if drop-back passer protection develops, will be most likely picked up by the offensive right guard. In this stunt the guard should be his assigned key—not to react to for initial movement but for *secondary* reaction. The defensive lineman knows where he is going to charge, that is pre-determined, but as he begins his charge he needs a key to help him read the nature of the offensive play as it develops. If the play is a drop-back pass, he is on the desired route and all is well, but if the play is a running play, he possibly needs to make an adjustment in his charge or he may overshoot the action.

Presume that as the tackle loops, the right guard pulls to his right. (Diagram 3-10). Indications are that the developing play will be a run to the offensive right, so the tackle, keying the guard, can now bring his charge under control and re-direct it toward the ball.

The stunting lineman or linebacker may sometimes find himself charging directly into the block of his key. In this case he

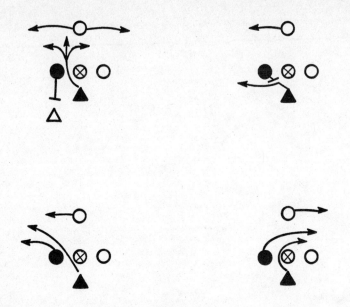

Diagram 3-11

will fight pressure, find the football and pursue. Diagrams 3-11, 3-12 and 3-13 illustrate secondary reactions and pursuit of the middle guard, tackles and inside linebackers of an Oklahoma defense.

Those defenders who will not be a part of the pass rush must be careful not to indicate this to the offensive blockers in advance. In Diagram 3-14 we see a pattern in which the right inside linebacker will drop off to a pass zone. If he tips this intention to the offensive left guard prior to the snap of the ball, it would be possible for the guard to drop back and turn to his outside immediately to give assistance to the left halfback.

Coaches frequently tell their linebackers to take a position farther off the line of scrimmage in obvious pass situations to be able to get into their pass coverage responsibility easier and more quickly. This may assist the linebackers in carrying out their assignments, but it compounds the problems of the pass rush unit. The uncovered offensive linemen can anticipate the rush and shift on the snap of the ball to the overload point. To avoid this the linebackers should either maintain a constant depth or continually vary their positions, keeping the offensive blockers always guessing as to what their true intentions are.

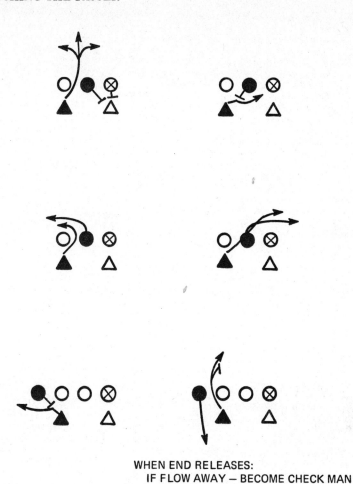

WHEN END RELEASES:
IF FLOW AWAY — BECOME CHECK MAN
IF QB DROPS — RUSH AND CONTAIN

Diagram 3-12

The standard footwork for performing the lineman's slant charge, so frequently used in overload pass rushing, is a quick two-step maneuver. From a head-up position or a slight outside position on the offensive man a defensive tackle would execute a penetrating slant to his inside as illustrated in Diagram 3-15a. He starts his charge with a fast diagonal step to his right with the left foot followed by a fast diagonal step with his right foot. His right shoulder is directed at the hip of the offensive lineman to his right. To protect his legs he uses an arm lift with his left arm as he takes his diagonal steps. These first two steps have moved him laterally,

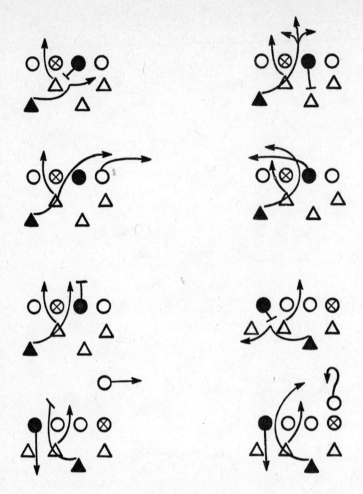

Diagram 3-13

and in his third and fourth steps he must turn his body so that his shoulders are parallel to the line of scrimmage, his body weight is forward, and his arms are in front of him as he directs his charge into the offensive backfield.

A variation of this standard slant charge, which I feel is quicker and more easily executed, is illustrated in Diagram 3-15b. I have always felt that on the first step of the standard charge, when the defender steps diagonally across the blocker's face, he is especially vulnerable since at the moment he is in an off-balance position. This alternate footwork avoids this position since the first step

Diagram 3-14

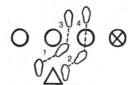

a.

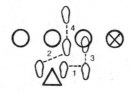

b.

Diagram 3-15

is a *lateral* step to the inside with the inside foot. Simultaneously, the lineman shifts his body weight to the inside fast and drives in the direction of the near hip of the next inside offensive lineman. Although his inside foot is moving laterally on this first step, his shoulders move diagonally toward the inside lineman. The second step is diagonal across the blocker's face, but by this time the inside foot is firmly planted and providing a base to absorb any blow from the outside blocker. Since the defender's body has not been turned at the hips to make this maneuver, he can now square his shoulders with the line of scrimmage more quickly and follow through with his charge.

Playing the overload principle in pass rush is essentially a stunting game and it should be kept in mind that stunting is a gamble. When the defensive captain calls for an overload to rush the passer, he is first of all gambling that the quarterback will call a pass. If the play turns out to be a run away from the overload, the defensive pursuit is somewhat impaired since the stunting players will be moving away from the ball. If the called play is a run attempt into the overload, however, the stunt will probably be very effective in stopping it.

Except in certain pass situations and when positive tendencies of specific opponents may make it feasible, it is generally advisable *not* to stunt into the short side of the field from a hash-mark position. Unless there are sound reasons for it, based upon adequate scouting reports, it is not sound football to stunt on the weak side of a heavy formation, particularly if that set is to the open side of the field. (Diagram 3-16).

By developing a set of principles such as the above, based upon knowledge of your opponent and providing them to your defensive signal caller, some of the gamble can be taken from the overload system of pass rush. Emphasize the need for all-out effort in the rush and the deep men should be able to cover their receivers closer because of the pressure on the quarterback

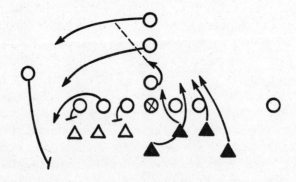

Diagram 3-16

INDIVIDUAL TECHNIQUE

Only a few years ago I recall hearing one of our prominent college coaches say, "Trying to rush the passer wastes more effort than any phase of line play." If that statement is still a part of his philosophy, it may account for the fact that his teams haven't been doing so well in the recent years of the "passing era." Too frequently we have neglected this phase of football or have not really been specific in our instructions as to *how* to rush the passer. We tend to gloss over the techniques of pass rushing by giving our players vague directions such as, "When you see the quarterback drop back to pass, put on a hard rush and come in with your arms high." I will agree that players equipped with no more instructions than that probably are doing little more than wasting effort.

I believe that one of the skills of football most difficult to master is offensive blocking, and one of the most difficult blocks is the passer protection block. If this is true, then the passer protection cup is vulnerable to defensive linemen who will spend the necessary time to master the techniques of destroying the dropback blocker. A pass rush based on a one-on-one match between rusher and blocker should be successful at least 50 percent of the time, other considerations being equal, but we all know that in most contests today the blockers are winning the battles. Why? I think the answer is simple. Those coaches who rely on individual technique, with occasional red-dog assistance, do not allocate enough practice time to the skills of shedding a passer protection blocker. Likewise, those coaches who rely on the overload principle spend too much time coaching a variety of stunts and rushing patterns and not enough time working with the individual rusher. When he gets to the overload point he doesn't know what to do.

The coach with a good passer and a good pass offense would like to achieve a balanced attack of equal running and passing. He knows that the only way to accomplish this proficiency in both phases of offense is to devote as much practice time to his pass offense as he does to his running offense. He also knows that his quarterback cannot throw while reclining on the seat of his pants, so he makes certain that his offensive linemen receive hours and hours of work in passer protection blocking. Here is his advantage as a pass-minded coach. While he allocates 50 percent of his offensive practice time to pass offense, he knows that it will be a rare opponent that allocates 50 percent of his defensive practice time to pass defense. The result is a well trained, proficient group of offensive linemen, skilled in passer protection blocking, opposed by a unit of defensive linemen and linebackers whose total pass-rush practice time has been minimal.

Training the pass rusher starts with making him pass conscious. Emphasize to him the importance of anticipating the pass play, drill him on always being aware of the game situation, and school him on the opponent's pass tendencies. He needs to be taught to look for pass indications every time he takes his position on the line of scrimmage. He should study the stance of the offensive blocker as the game progresses, he may vary his foot position in anticipation of a pass block. It is not unusual for offensive linemen to unconsciously close their splits down when a pass has been called. Sometimes the amount of weight on the blockers "down" hand is an indicator. If his weight is forward, he intends to fire out, straight ahead, and if his weight is back, he may be anticipating a drop-back passer protection block. If good game films of the opponents are available, the pass rushers should study them on their own time during the week looking for tip-offs and individual weaknesses that can be exploited. Those defensive linemen who can predict the drop-back pass each time it is called make their job immeasurably easier. They can dig their cleats in, predetermine the type of rush they intend to use and the maneuver that will best shed the passer protection blocker and give them a shot at Mr. Big, the quarterback.

Today we generally recognize four main types of block protection for defensive linemen: 1) rip-up, 2) hand shiver, 3) forearm block, and 4) the arm lift. A good all-around defensive lineman will master all four of these skills since they are applicable to the different responsibilities that may be assigned to him. To protect his "block zone," the area between his knees and his shoulders, and effect a control charge on his opponent in which he could release left or right, he would want to use the hand shiver. If he wants to control only the inside or the outside of an opponent, he might use the rip-up or the forearm block. Unless the defender is able to predict the pass play, he must be ready at the line of scrimmage for a run and consequently prepared to protect himself from the offensive blocker's charge with the appropriate block protection technique. As the play begins and he starts his own defensive charge, however, he has to modify his arm action if his opponent drops back for passer protection. The four basic block protection techniques used against runs are next to worthless against the passer protection blocker who is dropping away from rather than driving toward the defensive man.

The pass protection blocker sets up as quickly as he can, dropping off the line of scrimmage to a depth of one to two yards with his back turned slightly to the inside. His head is up, knees bent, and his arms held close to his body ready to hit when the defensive man drives into him. He attempts to maintain a wide base and keep his weight on the balls of his feet. The blocker waits until the rusher is practically upon him before he delivers his blow. With his feet moving in short, choppy steps he will uncoil on the defender with an upward movement hitting with head and arms together underneath the rusher's shoulder pads and headgear.

The objective of this short, powerful blow is to check the defender's momentum by knocking him back on his heels, forcing him to start his rush over again. In the meantime the blocker can set again and prepare himself for the next charge.

The blocker attempts to maintain his position with the inside foot back to prevent the rusher from collapsing him to the inside, while inviting the defender to the outside. If the rusher works to the outside, the blocker simply uses his own momentum to force him past the passer, keeping his own body between the rusher and the passer. If the rusher should decide to go to the inside, the offensive blocker will drop his outside foot back, turn his head to the inside across the rusher's path and drive him into the other blockers and rushers. This is the classic passer protection blocker. This is the opponent that the defensive pass rusher must overcome.

Whatever rush technique the defender decides to use in combating the blocker, it must be done with maximum speed and smoothness. Bear in mind that most passes will be on their way within three seconds after the snap of the ball. The techniques employed must be practiced and drilled until they become automatic reactions like counters in wrestling.

Let me emphasize again that the pass rush can be very effective without actually getting to the passer, although this should be the defender's primary goal. The pass blockers are attempting to maintain a clear area around the passer as indicated in Diagram 3-17. Whether the defender breaks into this area himself or he jams the blocker into it, the presence of bodies in this area

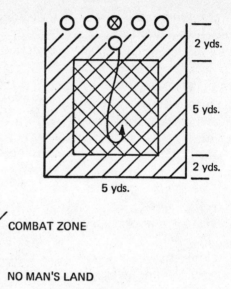

COMBAT ZONE

NO MAN'S LAND

Diagram 3-17

restricts the vision and the movement of the quarterback and possibly denies a desired line of flight for the intended pass. Some of the techniques of pass rush have been developed more for jamming than to accomplish a clean break of the rusher into "no man's land."

The Butt and Shiver

The most vulnerable aspect of the pass blocker's technique is his drop-back action as he shuffles backward to set up for the onslaught of the defender. It is during this movement that the blocker has his weight back and neither foot in a position to brace himself against the defender's charge. The butt and shiver technique is ideal for the attack under these circumstances; it is swift and simple. The prime requisite is the defender's ability to read and react instantly to the first backward movement of the blocker by driving hard and fast across the line of scrimmage. Direct the charge straight at the blocker, body weight well forward, with short, quick steps, and the arms extended in front. Gain contact as quickly as possible with the heels of the hands driving up and into the shoulder pads. As the blocker attempts to slow his backward movement to set himself for the uncoil, the rusher should lower his head and butt him with the helmet. This force should be strong enough to rock him back on his heels making it possible to drive him back into the passer.

Speed is mandatory in executing this technique. Contact must be made while the blocker is still moving backward into position so that the momentum of the rusher's charge will continue this backward movement, never allowing the blocker to get set.

Take-a-wing

Many offensive coaches teach the pass protection blocker to set up with the arms held high, fists in contact with the chest, upper arms parallel to the ground, and elbows extended outward to increase the blocking surface. Against this type of blocker the take-a-wing technique is especially effective.

The defender should drive directly at the middle of the blocker in an effort to make him set himself firmly, thereby reducing his mobility. This head-on rush also allows the defender to execute the take-a-wing on the inside or outside, whichever presents the best opportunity.

Assuming that the rusher is a defensive left tackle who intends to maneuver to the outside of the blocker, his first movement would be an all-out charge to the offensive man. At the point of contact he would drive the blocker's outside elbow high by striking it upward with the heel of his left hand and at the same time grabbing the elbow with that hand, forcing it higher while shoving the blocker to the inside. This must be accomplished quickly in one continuous movement while the right forearm strikes a rip-up blow to the blocker's chest. The rusher's body weight must be well forward on the balls of his feet, leaning into the blocker throughout this technique. As the offensive man is over-balanced to his inside, the rusher continues the upward and inward pressure on the blocker's outside elbow as he takes a lateral step to the outside with his left foot and then re-directs his charge, moving to the outside of the blocker.

Ideally, in this example the tackle would make contact with his inside foot forward, pointing directly to the middle of the blocker. The feet should never be planted, however, and must be kept free and moving constantly to allow the rusher to take advantage of any opportunity that may present itself.

The Judo Technique

In this maneuver, the rusher again charges directly at the offensive man attempting to influence him to dig in his cleats, and get braced to meet the charge. As the rusher approaches, he reaches with his right hand across the blocker's chest grabbing the top of his right shoulder, then as he closes with the blocker he drives his right forearm under the chin and immediately applies an upward leverage forcing the blocker's head upward and backward. This action, combined with a hard upward blow to the ribs with the heel of the left hand, will rock the offensive man's weight back on his heels making it possible to power him backward into the passer protection cup.

The Run-around

One of the simplest techniques is the run-around which is best employed against a blocker who lacks agility and quick feet. The rusher freezes the blocker with a head-on rush, but just before contact he turns his head out and steps across in front of the offensive man with his inside foot and drops his inside shoulder to absorb the block. The inside forearm is carried low across the body at waist level to assist in protecting the rusher's block zone and to push away from the blocker as the maneuver is completed.

Slip Technique

If the defender can rush directly at the offensive man anticipating an even block pressure, then the slip technique can be effective, particularly when the defender has a height advantage.

The rusher's inside leg should be forward as he turns his head out and grabs the blocker's outside shoulder with both hands. Maintaining pressure on the blocker, he presses down on this shoulder while turning his own hips and shoulders to the outside, and slips sideways past the blocker.

Club Technique

Outside rushers can frequently get their opponent to shuffle out by directing their charge to the outside shoulder, and when contact is made, the blocker will usually attempt to maintain an outside block pressure hoping to drive the rusher past the quarterback.

The club technique is a simple device for use in this situation. As the offensive man begins to shuffle out, the rusher should take a quick diagonal step to the inside with the inside foot and club him with the inside forearm just below the shoulder pads. This blow must be delivered with the fist doubled up to tighten and harden the forearm muscles and should be thrown with force, driving off the inside leg. The outside hand should be used to push the opponent's helmet to the outside and aid in breaking contact with the blocker as the defender now turns to the inside.

The Stiff Arm

For many years the stiff arm was a favorite tool of the broken field runner. However, with the power and improved tackling techniques of present day defensive players it has fallen into disrepute. And now it is a part of the pass rusher's technique.

If an outside rusher directs his charge to the outside shoulder of the pass protection blocker and the offensive man does not shuffle out, the stiff arm technique can be used to good advantage. The rusher delivers a hard blow to the outside of the opponent's head with the heel of his inside hand. This should be timed so that the elbow is slightly bent at the time of contact but is straightened and locked an instant later during the follow-through. At the same time the outside hand should strike the blocker's outside elbow forcing it across his chest. Now the stiff arm will have glanced off the blocker's helmet and be in position for the rusher to reach over the blocker's back and pull him to the inside while he continues his outside charge.

If the blocker is over-enthusiastic about shuffling to the outside when the rusher initially charges at his outside shoulder, the defensive man can merely reverse this technique and go to the inside. When the blocker works wide, the rusher delivers the stiff arm with the heel of his outside arm to the inside of the blocker's helmet, pushes the inside elbow across his chest, and pushes and pulls him out while taking an inside route to the passer.

The Fake and Roll-out

The fake and roll-out technique can be used to the inside or the outside of the blocker but it must be done smoothly and quickly since it develops more slowly than the other techniques. A successful roll-out is quite worthless if the pass has been thrown by the time the defender breaks clear of his blocker.

Once again the rusher should drive directly at the pass protection blocker pressuring him to set up and dig in. It is imperative that the rusher put on a hard charge with maximum forward body lean. If the rusher intends to fake out and roll inside, he should take a quick diagonal step to the outside with his outside foot and throw his head to the outside just before contact is made. On his next step he drives his inside foot toward the middle of the blocker as he strikes a powerful rip-up blow to the numbers with his inside forearm and a hand shiver to the blocker's outside shoulder with his own outside hand. If his charge has rocked the offensive man backward, he should drive against him for two more steps maintaining pressure to the outside, but if he has met solid resistance, he should go into his roll technique immediately. The roll is accomplished by dropping the outside hand quickly, releasing the pressure on the blocker's outside shoulder while maintaining the pressure on the inside shoulder with the forearm. This will cause the blocker to turn his shoulders slightly inward as the rusher begins the roll by dropping his outside foot back and to the inside. This must be a good-sized step which places the foot at least even with the inside foot of the blocker. A heavy pressure must be maintained on the blocker's inside shoulder since that contact now becomes the pivot point for the roll. The rusher drops his hips slightly, turns his head and shoulders away from the blocker and shifts his weight to the back foot while shoving away from the blocker at the last instant with what had been his inside forearm. As he disengages, he swings his hips around to the inside and is in position to continue his charge to the passer.

The fake and roll can be worked to the inside or outside since the rusher is then on the most direct route to the passer when the roll is completed.

THE CONTAIN MEN

The outside rushers are the contain men and they are charged with the additional responsibility of not letting the quarterback break out of the protective cup to scramble to the outside. Depending upon the pattern of the rush, the contain men may be ends, tackles or linebackers on a red-dog route. They must maintain an outside leverage on the deepest cup protector on their side until the quarterback begins his forward slide motion into the cup. Once the quarterback steps into his cup it is difficult for him to pull back out and scramble to the outside.

The outside rusher should be careful to gain sufficient depth in the defensive backfield before he challenges the blocker. Coming in too shallow makes him vulnerable for a hook block by the protector, leaving the gate open for the quarterback on the outside. But because he does rush deeper before contact, the offensive blocker assigned to him must drop back deeper and faster to pick him up making the blocker vulnerable to a variety of rushing techniques, particularly the butt and shiver, which can carry his backward momentum on into the pass.

The contain man must also be alert for modern variations of the old Statue of Liberty Play, and unless a pre-determined technique that he wishes to employ dictates otherwise, he should always keep his outside foot free, enabling him to release from his blocker at any time and shuffle outside to assume his outside responsibility.

On reading a screen pass to his side, he should check his charge and go to the ball to be in position to make the tackle or block in case of an interception. If he has already charged in deep, he should continue his rush with hands up to obstruct the passer's view or force him to lob the ball high over him. If the screen is away from him, he should continue his charge on the passer to drop him or force him to hurry his throw. If the pass has been thrown before he can get to the passer, he should carry his charge through in the direction of the throw to possibly be in position to make the tackle or to block in the case of an interception.

In many types of passer protection blocking, a back will be assigned to pick up the outside rusher. This factor can often lead to mis-matches where a small running back is charged with the responsibility of blocking a much larger defensive man. When this opportunity presents itself, the defender should take advantage of it and drive through the back at full speed, punishing him physically as much as possible in the process. In fact, a little extra effort should be made in doing this early in the ball game and the rusher will find his task easier to accomplish during the remainder of the game. Since the backfield blocker can set up quickly, he is usually in a somewhat stationary position when contact is made. On the other hand, the outside rusher generally comes from some distance and has the opportunity to develop considerable speed and power prior to contact. Of course this technique cannot be done with reckless abandon—some small men are superb blockers, so the rusher needs to study his man carefully and be ready to employ other techniques if necessary.

Too frequently, contain men are content merely to contain. This is actually their *secondary* assignment in the pass rush unit; their first responsibility is to pressure the passer, and by virtue of their position, the visual field and freedom of movement it affords, they should be the most effective rushers. It is a mistake for contain men to think only in terms of containment. If a four-man rushing pattern is called and the two contain men are thinking only in terms of outside responsibility, then only two men are rushing.

The dual responsibility of the contain men plus the fact that they have support only to their inside makes it essential that these players have good speed and mobility. In working out stunting patterns to apply the overload principle of pass defense, the coach should be cautious that the players who are assigned to containment are physically capable of meeting the requirements.

Raising the Hands

A vital part of a good pass rush is raising the hands at the proper time. Most defensive linemen, however, have a tendency to raise them too early, and since the hands and arms are vital to combating the pass protection blockers, these linemen are neglecting that phase of the pass rush. The rusher should read the quarterback while he fights the blocker, and train himself to avoid reacting to the quarterback's fakes. Most good quarterbacks have been taught to carry the ball at chest height with both hands until they are ready to throw, and when making fakes or "flags," with the ball, they tend to leave the left hand high and pound the ball into it at the end of the fake pass motion. Linemen should learn to recognize this arm action and raise their hands only when the passer pulls his left hand away and begins a long arm movement with the ball.

Many linemen feel that the reason for raising their hands is to knock the ball down or to intercept it. Of course this is what we would always like to do but it seldom happens. Extending the arms high over the head obstructs both the passer's and the receiver's view. Many passers are bothered while trying to look through a maze of extended arms and have a tendency to overthrow their short passes and underthrow the long passes.

Raising the hands forces a high pass, and the higher the pass, the longer the ball is in the air and the more distance the defense can cover in reacting to it. The high, long pass has a tendency to "hang" and fall short while the high, short pass has a tendency to float and overshoot its mark.

The short hitch, hook, and slant passes must be thrown on a line to be effective and the ball must be delivered quickly before the pass defenders can react to it. In throwing the hook pass for example, if the passer is forced to arch the ball to clear the raised hands of the pass rushers, he will either overthrow his receiver or throw so softly that the, inside linebackers will have little trouble moving laterally to play the ball in front of the receiver. If the rusher reaches the passer, he should tackle him high stripping him from the top down, pinning his arms to the side if possible. This technique frequently results in a fumble if the passer has dropped his left hand away and has begun his pass action at the time of contact. When another rusher has already made high contact, the next man should come in at waist level to insure against the passer ducking under the arms of the high tackler. When coming in from the blind side, one should consider the possibility of taking the ball away from the passer as well as making him cough it up with a high vicious tackle.

THE RUSHING UNIT

The greatest danger in rushing the passer is failure of the defensive man to maintain the proper relationship in the rushing pattern. Everyone must stay within a designated lane, not only to avoid vulnerability to draw plays but also to restrict the

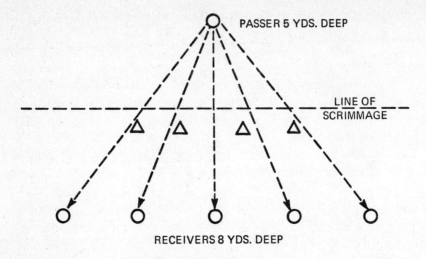

PASSER 5 YDS. DEEP

LINE OF
SCRIMMAGE

RECEIVERS 8 YDS. DEEP

Diagram 3-18

quarterback's field of vision and force him to throw in narrow cor-
ridors between the lanes.

After illustrating on the blackboard the concept of coordinated rushing lanes, the coach can emphasize the importance and
advantage of this principle with the following drill. Align the unit
on a line of scrimmage in one of their rushing patterns. Place
receivers between the rushers at a depth of 7-8 yards and station a
quarterback in an imaginary cup, having him throw between the
rushers while they attempt to bat or intercept the ball. (Diagram
3-18). After a dozen throws, converge the rushers to within three
yards of the passer and repeat the throw pointing out the significance of a hard penetrating rush with everyone staying within his
assigned lane. With arms extended, the rushers, while still three
yards away, present a formidable "picket fence" to the passer and
make it difficult for him to throw effectively in the narrow spaces
between them, making it necessary to throw high or loft the ball
over their outstretched arms.

Of course the first priority for the rushing unit is to get the
quarterback before he can throw the ball. All of the variety of
rushing patterns that a team employs must be walked through,
rehearsed in dummy drill, and practiced in full speed contact work
to perfect the coordination and timing essential to a good pass rush.
To provide this contact opportunity for the rushers and yet
minimize the injury possibilities to the pass protection blockers, I

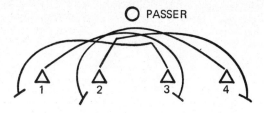

Diagram 3-19

have found it a good practice to put blocking aprons, rip pads, and the large forearm defensive pads on my offensive men. Besides the protection afforded, this equipment also slows down the offensive personnel sufficiently to provide an instructional advantage to the defense. By putting colored scrimmage jerseys on the quarterbacks and having a no-tackle rule, we can protect them from constant pounding. Sometimes, so we can carry through the drill, we move it in front of a hanging tackling dummy which substitutes for a quarterback. But it is my contention that the pass rush unit must work in addition at least 15 to 20 minutes each week, full speed under game conditions, to perfect its patterns and team work, and this contact should be the climax of the week's pass defense preparations for the next opponent.

Despite all efforts, the passer will still get most of his passes away, so a good drill to emphasize second effort by the rushers is essential. Too frequently in games, pass rushers come to a halt and become spectators after the pass has been thrown. Unfortunately when one of those passes goes awry and is intercepted, they are still spectators while the hapless interceptor scrambles about trying to pick his way through a host of tacklers. The drills illustrated in Diagrams 3-19 and 3-20 apply two popular approaches to organizing the second efforts of the pass rush unit. In Diagram 3-19 the rushers carry their charge through to the opposite side of the field putting them in position to block for an interceptor breaking to either sideline. This drill is appropriate for those defensive units in which the backs are trained to maneuver to the sideline after they make an interception.

A more recent philosophy is predicated on the belief that the interceptor will make more yardage if he breaks directly upfield instead of running laterally toward the sideline. Conforming with this idea, the pass rushers are taught to divert their charge in

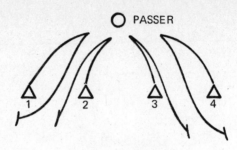

Diagram 3-20

the direction of the pass and peel-back block to their respective sides to open up a lane in the middle of the field. The drill illustrated in Diagram 3-20 develops this unit reaction.

Additional drill should be provided to the unit to acquaint them with the type of draw plays the next opponent employs. The rushers must know what their responsibilities are for draws and screens and be given practice experience in defending them. In all unit work the coach must constantly emphasize fundamentals, noting errors and making corrections. The rusher's steps should be short and quick, avoiding long strides that will extend him and thereby reduce his mobility. Teamwork and morale are vital to the pass rush unit. Too often, defensive linemen think that pass situations are a time for them to get some rest. There must be no "let-up," when the pass situation exists, they must think in terms of *attack*. If the pass rush unit can maintain a constant pressure on the passer, the defensive backs can cover the receivers more closely making the entire pass defense more effective.

Chapter 4

COACHING THE SECOND LINE OF PASS DEFENSE— DELAY OF RECEIVERS

The second line of defense against the passing attack is to delay the receivers. Defensive players, particularly ends and linebackers, can give pass receivers considerable difficulty in releasing from the line of scrimmage and getting into their desired pass routes. Receivers may be blocked, jammed, or shoved until the ball is in the air. Since all offensive players are potential blockers until the ball is thrown, the defensive players are privileged by the rules to use their hands against the receivers. They cannot be held, but even a momentary delay may contribute considerably to the total pass defense on a given down.

The importance of anticipating the pass situation must again be impressed upon the defensive team, They must be thoroughly familiar with the opponent's pass tendencies so that the delaying tactics can be applied at the proper time. Too frequently, delaying tactics have been reserved for the third-and-long-yardage situations, but in this day of flexible offenses, split receivers, and pass-minded coaches the pass is no longer a third-and-long-yardage weapon. To be most effective the delay of receivers should be applied frequently and not only in the most obvious pass situations.

There are four objectives in delaying a receiver but the most desirable is to eliminate him entirely. If he cannot run his pattern, the secondary will not have to cover him and the quarterback will be unable to throw to him. Nothing is guaranteed to shock a quarterback more than the sight of his primary receiver lying on the ground.

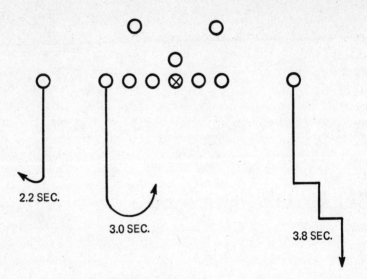

Diagram 4-1

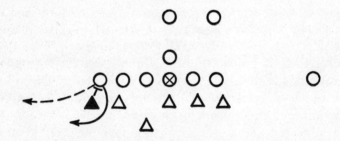

Diagram 4-2

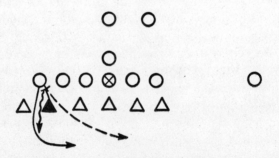

Diagram 4-3

More frequently, the delay is employed to disrupt the timing of the pass pattern. A good pass offense is a timed pass offense, with the quarterback and his receivers functioning with splitsecond precision. Diagram 4-1 illustrates the time elements for three typical short, medium, and long pass routes. The quarterback must be set to throw in 1.5–1.7 seconds. If we can destroy the rhythm of the pass play by temporarily interrupting the receiver, the defense gains a measure of advantage.

A third objective of delaying tactics may be to deny the receiver an intended route. In Diagram 4-2, the tight end has been called on a quick release to the outside but the outside backer has taken a tight position on his outside, shoving him to the inside to force him into a circuitous route to the defensive backfield. From an Eagle defense in Diagram 4-3, the inside backer has taken an inside position on the tight end who has been called on an across pattern. The backer, after a solid rip-up on the end, can maintain his inside position bumping and shoving him as he drops back to his own zone responsibility.

Anything that the defense can do which will force the passer to take longer to throw will increase the effectiveness of the pass rush. The fourth objective of delaying techniques is to augment the pass rush. The time requirements of the offensive passer protection blockers are difficult enough to achieve under normal circumstances against a hard rush, but when additional split seconds of quarterback protection are required because his receivers have been delayed, the burden may be too great and the rushers will be successful.

PRINCIPLES OF DELAY

Scouting reports should indicate who the favorite receivers are and their most effective routes. In establishing the delay plan for a given opponent, concentrate on the one or two dangerous receivers. Remember, however, that while the defensive man is bumping and shoving the receivers, he too is being delayed from performing his usual assignment. A defensive end may be in good position to jam a tight end or wingback, but if his primary responsibility is outside pass rush, then his effectiveness in the rush will be reduced by the time necessary to do the jamming. To attempt to delay all receivers is not sound defense nor is it necessary. One of the principles of war is "economy of force": do not use more combat power than is necessary to attain the objective. Applying this principle to the delay plan in pass defense, do not assign more defenders to delay responsibilities than are necessary to achieve the desired result *most of the time*. The more people assigned to delay, the less effective the rush or the coverage will be. If only the one or two favorite receivers are delayed, the potential for a powerful rush or effective coverage is conserved, yet the odds are favorable that the delay will also be effective.

Football is a game of percentages, and in pass defense as in other phases of the game we would like to force our opponent to do things that he normally does not do. If we can delay those receivers to whom the quarterback normally throws the greatest percentage of passes, we force him to look for his secondary receivers and consequently can presume that his pass offense will be less successful.

Those defenders assigned to delay receivers should have two responsibilities in the pass defense play. It is difficult to delay a determined receiver for an extended period of time and such a delay is seldom necessary anyhow; consequently the defenders should have a second assignment in the pass defense. The purposes of delay are often achieved in the first second or two after the snap of the ball, and after the receiver has finally released, the defender should react to a secondary responsibility of pass rush or pass coverage. If this responsibility is coverage, quite often the defender has the opportunity to continue harassing the receiver as he drops back into his zone or moves into position to pick up his assigned receiver.

The delay plan must be coordinated with the rush and coverage plans. It is impossible to emphasize all three at once since several players will have separate responsibilities in each phase. Consequently the coach must build into his defensive alignment and coverage systems the emphasis that he desires. The defensive team captain or signal caller can then apply the pass defense pressure that he wants from play to play merely by calling the alignments or the coverage pattern. Some defensive patterns will be designed to provide a strong pass rush, some will emphasize coverage, and others will provide effective delay of receivers.

INDIVIDUAL TECHNIQUES

Defensive tackles, ends, and linebackers are most often in the best position to obstruct pass receivers. Tight receivers playing on the line of scrimmage present three possibilities for delay by a single defender: (1) delay and force an inside release; (2) delay and force an outside release; (3) delay and obstruct release to either side.

For these purposes, two techniques have proven effective: the rip-up and drive; and jamming. In the performance of both of these it is essential to crowd the line of scrimmage to facilitate immediate contact with the receiver. It is also necessary to take a position that favors accomplishing the objective. If denial of the outside release is desired, then the defender should align himself in a position slightly outside the receiver; if an inside release is to be denied, then he should take an inside position. Many factors determine *exactly* how far outside or inside the offensive man a specific defender should play. The relative quickness of defender and receiver, the area of responsibility the defender has for the running game, and the defender's ability to avoid the offensive hook block are all considerations that a coach must weigh. I have found a shoulder-to-shoulder relationship (inside shoulder to outside shoulder) to be the maximum offset in which the defensive man can consistently make good contact. Helmet inside or outside is better, and the eye-to-eye relationship (inside eye to outside eye) is best if the defensive man can handle it without being hooked.

In both techniques the defensive principle of maintaining the shoulders in a position parallel to the line of scrimmage should be followed. This position, of course, maintains the defender's mobility and assists him in reacting to cross-blocks, traps and double-teams.

The Rip-Up and Drive

Since quickness is vital to assuring solid contact, the defender taking a position on a tight receiver, whether he is a lineman or linebacker, should have the foot forward that corresponds to the forearm with which contact will be made. If the defensive man has taken an outside position on the receiver, then he will be in a slightly staggered stance with the inside foot toward the receiver's crotch and ready to strike the rip-up blow to the numerals with inside foot and forearm. Body lean should be well forward as he drives off the outside foot.

If the defensive man's secondary assignment is pass rush, then an effort should be made to drive the receiver back off the line of scrimmage, maintaining contact as long as possible. If the defensive man's secondary assignment is pass coverage, then he should maintain his outside position after the initial contact and hand fight the receiver as long as he can while retreating into position for his pass coverage assignment.

The rip-up and drive technique is especially advisable when there is an equal possibility of a pass or run and the defender has an area responsibility corresponding to the side of the receiver on which he takes his position. If the potential receiver becomes a blocker for a running play, the rip-up charge is strong enough to neutralize the block and will afford a quick reaction to the ball. This technique should not be employed from a head-on position where the defender has running responsibility to both sides of the offensive man. The nature of the footwork and forearm action, driving to contact from the same side, favors taking an offset position.

Jamming

Whether head-on or offset, jamming is a useful technique in delaying receivers and has the additional value of being effective against split receivers. From a head-on position against a tight receiver the action is identical to the play of a middle guard using the two-hand shiver. With a toe-to-instep foot position, legs down well under him, the defender drives into the receiver striking an upward blow with the heels of the hands to the opponent's shoulders. The wrists and elbows should be locked at contact and a steady pressure maintained. The feet must be kept well spread so the defender can shuffle left or right in response to the offensive man's efforts to release or gain a blocking position.

The head-on defensive position implies running responsibility to both sides of the offensive man and the two-hand shiver is the best defensive technique to employ in this situation. It is also most ideal for jamming the receiver when there is no preference for forcing a release to one side or the other. While the rip-up and drive technique is most appropriate when the secondary responsibility is pass rush, the head-on jam technique is most appropriate when the secondary responsibility is pass coverage. If the defender keeps his legs back and away from his opponent after the initial contact, he will be in good position to maintain contact and continue to delay and obstruct the receiver as he "rides" him back into the defensive backfield while dropping off himself to his pass coverage responsibility.

From a position shading the inside or the outside of the receiver, jamming is also effective. In this situation the foot adjacent to the receiver should be forward and a short jab step taken with it toward the offensive man's crotch. Contact should be made with the heels of the hands, one against the side of the helmet and one against the opponent's shoulder. This should be a hard, jolting blow for the purpose of turning or twisting the receiver as he attempts to come off the line of scrimmage, momentarily delaying him and breaking his stride. With equal facility the defender can now carry out a pass rush assignment or drop back for pass coverage while continuing to harass the receiver.

The rip-up and drive would be hazardous to employ against a quick and agile split receiver; however, the techniques of jamming are more easily applied. Since most split men are now assuming a stand-up position, the defender should do likewise and his jamming technique will be somewhat different from that employed against a tight receiver. These modifications are covered in this chapter in the section which details delaying of wide receivers.

DELAYING THE RUNNING BACKS

There are three basic types of defensive end play (Diagram 4-4): (1) the Oklahoma style; (2) boxing; and (3) crashing. In the box and crash styles, the end with outside rush and contain responsibility can also be effective in delaying the running back when he attempts to release to the outside for pass patterns. The Oklahoma style end is less effective in this assignment since his line of scrimmage contact delays him.

In the box technique, the near back should be assigned as the end's key. As "pass" shows and the back starts to his side, the end can adjust to him while getting depth into the offensive backfield. A back releasing to the outside on pass patterns has only

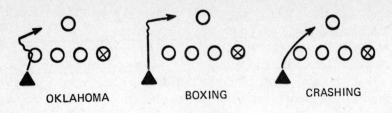

OKLAHOMA   BOXING   CRASHING

Diagram 4-4

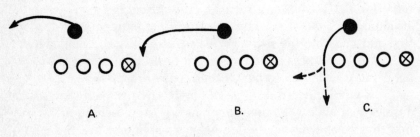

A.   B.   C.

Diagram 4-5

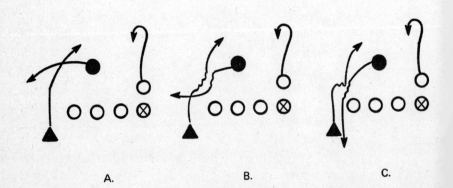

A.   B.   C.

Diagram 4-6

three routes available (Diagram 4-5). He can "belly" back as in
running a swing pass (A), move directly toward the sideline to get
width before turning upfield (B), or drive just outside the defensive
tackle for a route upfield or a quick break into the flat (C).

While moving across the line of scrimmage, the boxing end
reads the near back. If he sets up for pass protection, the end
begins his normal outside contain rush, but if the back moves on
one of the three pass release routes and the end has been assigned
delay responsibility, then he must adjust slightly to the movement
of the back (Diagram 4-6). If the back swings, the end continues his
pass rush as it will be almost impossible to contact him and continue an effective pass rush. If the back moves laterally to the
sideline, the boxing end is in an ideal position to cut him off and rip
him with the inside forearm. He must get his depth first, then step
into the back with his inside leg forward, keep his outside leg free,
and not get tied up. To avoid the possibility of being hooked in, the
end should force the back to release to his inside.

When the back attempts an off-tackle release, the end can
close down from the outside and jam him to the inside. Again,
contact should be made with the inside leg forward so the outside
leg can remain free, allowing the end to quickly disengage and
continue on his outside rush and contain charge.

The boxing end must constantly be reminded that the delay
responsibility is secondary to his assignments of rush and contain.
He must not move out of his normal rushing lane to chase the
backfield receiver.

The crashing end also keys the near back. He should charge
to a point one yard outside the back's near hip. Along this line he
can readily adjust to the back's release route and "get a piece of
him." As the end begins his charge on the snap of the ball, he
should watch the back's feet. His first two steps will tell the end
what his intentions are—pass protection or pass release, and if the
charge is hard and fast, as this type must be, the end will be
successful in contacting the back regardless of the direction of the
pass release.

Some pass offenses emphasize the inside tackle release of
backs into the pass pattern (Diagram 4-7). The advantages of disguise and surprise are apparent, and if these receivers are freely
allowed to break into the defensive backfield, the pass defense will
have many anxious moments as uncovered receivers seemingly
appear from nowhere.

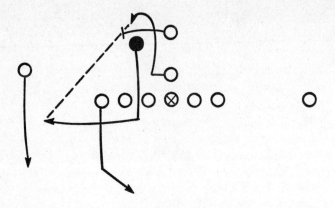

Diagram 4-7

The defensive interior linemen and linebackers must be brought into the delaying plan to combat this tactic. Scouting reports and film analysis should indicate the favorite release avenues of the dangerous backs. What maneuvers do they use to break through the interior line? Which defensive holes do they penetrate? Having the answer to these questions, the pass defense coach can assign a man-to-man delay responsibility to each appropriate lineman or linebacker. On pass situations, then, these defenders will play their normal responsibilities and also key their assigned back. If he attempts to come through their territorial assignments, they will step into him and deliver a powerful blow before continuing their normal pass defense responsibilities.

The back releasing inside tackle is generally not hitting this area with the power that he normally would if he were carrying the ball. He tends to be more upright and attempts to pick his way through the defense rather than blast through. These factors make him more vulnerable to the punishment that only interior defensive linemen and linebackers can deliver, and nothing in their bag of tricks is more punishing than the double forearm rip and the clothesline technique. Either of these blows, if delivered just as the back reaches the line of scrimmage, can set him backward on the turf, eliminating him as an effective receiver and discouraging him from taking that route again.

DELAYING THE WIDE RECEIVERS

The manner in which split ends and split backs are utilized in some spread type formations makes it advisable to place a defen-

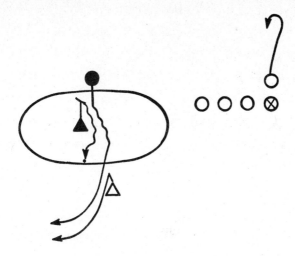

Diagram 4-8

sive man with delay responsibility on some of these potential receivers. Sometimes the need is to delay and assist in the coverage
of an outstanding receiver. In Diagram 4-8, the defensive end has a
delay responsibility on the split halfback and will cover the flat
zone after the halfback releases. The corner back picks up the
receiver man-for-man as he clears the end, so in effect this maneuver is a form of double coverage with a delay.

Some coaches do not like to assign a delay man to a wide
receiver because they feel he is too isolated to contribute to the
running defense. If the game situation strongly indicates pass, they
are willing to sacrifice an extra man to gain double coverage on an
especially dangerous receiver, but otherwise they prefer not to
spread their primary defense. This philosophy is sound if the offense has a powerful inside-tackle attack and a weak or mediocre
outside attack, but many teams that employ split backs and ends
have developed not only outstanding pass offenses, but also
dangerous outside running attacks utilizing the split men as key
crack-back blockers (Diagram 4-9). Against this type of offense,
spreading an inside linebacker or end with the split man actually
assists the running defense as well as placing a man in position who
is able to delay the receiver and cover the flat zone on passes.

The man assigned to delay a wide receiver should take a
tight stand-up position on the line of scrimmage. Whether he takes
an inside, outside, or head-on position will depend on his primary
responsibility in the total run-pass defensive scheme, how wide the
receiver is split, and the favorite routes of that receiver.

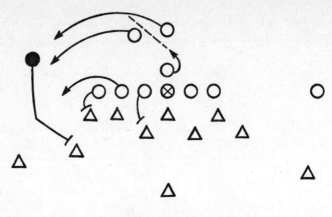

Diagram 4-9

If he has outside running responsibility against the ground game, then he will generally abide by the common "split rules": maintain an outside position on a split man until he moves out to 7 yards; move head-up at 7-8 yards; and move to an inside position beyond 8 yards. The outside position on short splits denies the offensive man the opportunity to drive the defender to the inside for power sweeps and quick tosses.

The leg nearer the receiver should be forward, splitting the crotch of his opponent. If the split man is an end, then the defender can crowd him on the line of scrimmage, carrying most of his body weight on the forward foot.

His key is the quarterback, while watching the receiver with peripheral vision. It is of the utmost importance that the defender *not* focus his attention on the split man. With a little practice he can learn to "feel" this man while reading the quarterback and the ball for indications of pass or run. It must be emphasized that the defender is *not assigned* to the split receiver for coverage; his job is merely to delay the receiver then assume a second responsibility.

On the snap of the ball, the defender must step into the split man with his near foot. If he makes good contact, he should maintain it, driving the man back off the line of scrimmage, while watching the quarterback and the development of the play. If a pass is indicated, an excellent delay has been effected and now the defender can continue to bump and shove the split receiver while he backs out to cover the flat zone. If a run develops away from him, he can release from the contact and move back into rotation, watching for a reverse or a throwback pass. If a sweep develops toward him, he is in excellent position to assume outside running responsibility and begin to pinch in on the play, forcing the runner to cut inside and into the pursuit pattern.

The characteristics of the wide receiver dictate the specific method of contact the defender can employ. Most split men are fast and agile so the two-hand jamming shiver may be the only blow that can be delivered if they are releasing for a pass. On the other hand not many split receivers are properly prepared to meet delay men on the line of scrimmage. The tactic is not very common and coaches tend to overlook the need to give these men the same practice experience that is given tight ends in releasing down field. If that is the case, the defender may be surprised to find that he can occasionally deliver a very effective rip-up.

Delay Techniques for Inside Linebackers

The extent to which the inside linebackers can be effectively utilized in the delay of receivers depends upon the team defensive alignments employed. Linebackers can perform a delay responsibility on the line of scrimmage as in a Pro-43 defense or in an Eagle 52 defense (Diagram 4-10), or they can be effective downfield in delaying receivers who attempt to pass through the short interior zones.

When delaying a tight receiver at the line of scrimmage, the linebacker uses the same techniques of rip-up and jamming that have been previously described for linemen. However, he has an additional tactic that can be used occasionally—the body block. If the defensive alignment will allow him to take a position a yard or two on either side of the receiver, he will have a good angle to drop the receiver with a low body block. An agile linebacker can easily perform this task and still scramble to his feet and adequately cover a short interior pass zone. This tactic is not recommended for frequent use, but can be extremely valuable in critical "sure pass" situations. The possibility of a running play must be remote since the linebacker must commit himself immediately. A surprise element must be maintained so that the receiver is concentrating on his route rather than his block protection.

The Eagle defense provides an exceptionally good opportunity for the inside linebacker and end to double team a tight offensive end. Their positions in this alignment allow them to put a

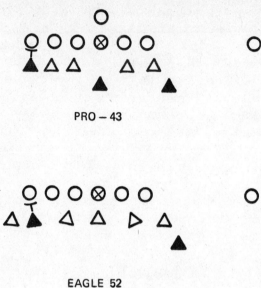

PRO – 43

EAGLE 52

Diagram 4-10

very effective pinch on the receiver, making it difficult for him to release from the line of scrimmage.

Interior linebackers playing the short center zones are in an excellent position for delaying receivers who attempt to route into or through these areas. A detailed discussion of these techniques is presented in Chapter 6, "Defending the Short Passing Zones."

The Bump and Run

Many teams that employ man-for-man pass defense have incorporated the "bump and run" technique into their systems. In reality, this method of pass defense is a combination of delay and cover by a single defender. A careful analysis of this technique will be presented in Chapter 8, "Individual Man-For-Man."

Chapter 5

COACHING THE
DEEP ZONE DEFENDERS

Many coaches feel that the zone type of pass defense most nearly achieves perfection in pass coverage. Although the man-for-man is growing increasingly popular in high school and college football, its demanding personnel requirements still leave the zone as the most frequently employed in other than the professional ranks.

Although two-deep and four-deep zone defenses have gained a significant foothold in many pass defense systems, the three-deep style remains the basic zone coverage scheme. This coverage is based upon the premise that three deep defenders can cover the deep zones from sideline to sideline. Since a football field is 53 yards wide, this means that each deep defender must be capable of laterally covering an area 17⅔ yards in width. The forward limits of the deep defenders' zones may vary from one coach to another, but 10 to 12 yards past the line of scrimmage is fairly standard. The rear limits of the deep zone extend naturally to the end line of the football field. The area between the deep zones and the line of scrimmage becomes the responsibility of the linebackers and ends. This area has traditionally been divided into four zones (Diagram 5-1). In most defensive alignments, sufficient personnel to man all four of these short zones will seldom be available, consequently one or more will usually be uncovered. The people assigned to the interior zones must be capable of covering a lateral distance of approximately 9 yards and to a depth of 12 yards.

The concept of zones and zone responsibility can best be illustrated by marking off a portion of the practice field in conform-

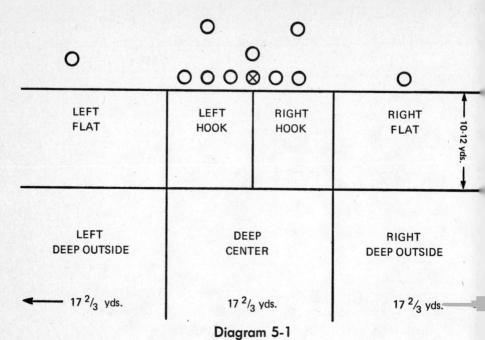

Diagram 5-1

ance with Diagram 5-1. Since a defender works in an area that will be his responsibility at game time, he needs a clear understanding of the boundaries of that area and an appreciation of its size and relationship to other zones. This is the single most important step in teaching zone pass defense. Have your players walk around the marked-off area as you identify each zone and its dimensions. Have your defensive backfield shift to their positions in each of your defensive alignments to illustrate the various zones for which they will be responsible. You will now have given them a brief "big picture" of a zone pass defense and they should be ready to begin their individual training.

BASIC PRINCIPLES OF ZONE COVERAGE

A few principles in zone coverage are applicable to all positions in the defensive backfield and should be kept in mind at all times:

1. On show of "pass" get depth in your zone, move to a point from which you can more easily cover your assigned territory.

2. Play the field and the ball—not the receiver.
3. Watch the passer. Receivers should be observed through peripheral vision.
4. Go to the ball when it is thrown. All backs, regardless of their position, must sprint to the ball as soon as it is thrown.

SELECTING THE THREE DEEP DEFENDERS

The most important positions in any zone defense are the deep defenders. These are the boys who constitute the last line of defense, who must prevent the cheap touchdown and must never let a receiver get behind them in their zone. The first priority in the selection of defensive personnel must rest in filling the positions in the three deep zones.

Height and speed are the ingredients that we would all like to have in our candidates for these positions. If we could order these boys from a catalog, we would also specify quick reaction time, ball-hawking ability, aggressiveness and a number of other desirable characteristics. Unfortunately, the high school or college coach must take what he can get, and sometimes only a few of these assets are apparent in the available candidates. Under these circumstances with which we are all familiar, it becomes necessary to determine which boys have the greatest potential, then get on with the business of training and developing that potential.

I once had the unique experience of coaching a major service football team which represented an installation with 30,000 troops assigned. When we put out a general call for football candidates, 250 reported. Our first task was to reduce the squad to the best 60 candidates within ten days, and to accomplish this my staff worked out a series of drills to evaluate players for various offensive and defensive positions. We had previously determined that we would basically use a three-deep zone defense, so the drills illustrated in Diagrams 5-2, 5-3, and 5-4, were set up to help us determine the best deep defenders. As a selective process these drills must have some merit since the top three players selected included one who had professional experience and two others who signed professional contracts after their service obligations were completed.

The running backwards drill should be set up at the sideline

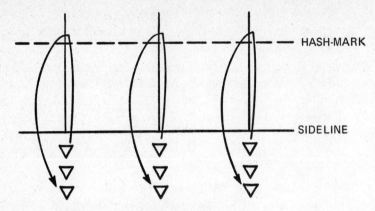

RUNNING BACKWARDS DRILL

Diagram 5-2

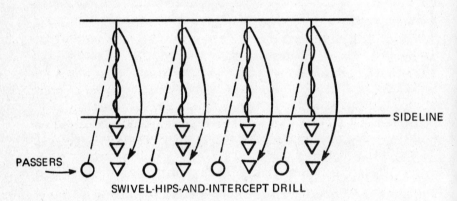

SWIVEL-HIPS-AND-INTERCEPT DRILL

Diagram 5-3

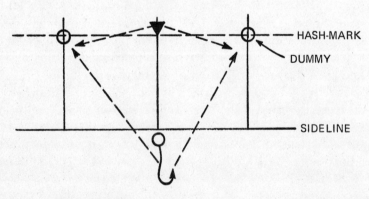

STRETCH DRILL

Diagram 5-4

with the boys divided into three or four groups positioned on five-yard line stripes. After a brief explanation and demonstration of good technique in running backwards (drop the hips, slight backward lean of the shoulders, do not throw the head back, etc.), have the boys run backwards down their respective five-yard line stripes to the hash-mark, then sprint forward to the sideline. Of 15 or 20 candidates in this drill, invariably two or three will fall down—forget them. Next put a stop watch on the remainder and extend the run to mid-field. Eliminate the slowest candidates and then move into the "swivel hips drill."

For this drill, add a quarterback to each line, stationing him about seven yards outside the sideline. Have the defensive back face the quarterback and begin running backwards down the line. The quarterback now pumps the ball as if to throw alternately to the receiver's left, then his right. With each simulated throw the defender turns his hips in that direction, does a cross-over step and continues to sprint down the line looking back over his shoulder, keeping his eyes on the quarterback. As a throw is faked to the opposite side, the defender rotates his hips and shoulders back toward the quarterback and into the new direction, never taking his eyes off the ball and continuing to sprint down the line.

Look for those boys who can accomplish these alternate turns at a high rate of speed and still run a fairly straight path down the five-yard stripe. Some boys will trip over their feet while turning, others will weave down the stripe, some will turn away from the quarterback, taking their eyes off the ball, and some will leave their hips facing toward the quarterback, running backwards while they merely rotate their shoulders left and right with the ball.

After each boy has had an opportunity to run this drill five or six times, add a little interest by having the quarterback throw the ball on the last turn. The back, on making the interception, should sprint full speed back to the sideline.

Finally in Diagram 5-4, I have illustrated the "stretch drill." Again, each of the three deep defenders must be capable of covering a lateral distance of 17⅔ yards, if as a unit they are going to be able to cover the deep area from sideline to sideline. This drill is designed for the purpose of determining the lateral capacity of each defender and then training him to extend or stretch that capacity.

Place helmets on top of two tall stand-up dummies on a hash-mark and ten yards apart. Have a defender station himself mid-way between the dummies. On the sideline have a quarterback simulate receiving the ball, then drop back seven yards, turn and throw to the helmet of one of the dummies which represent receivers. The defensive man must anticipate the release of the ball and move laterally at top speed to attempt an interception.

With the dummies only ten yards apart and at a depth of almost 18 yards from the line of scrimmage (sideline), the defender should have little difficulty in making the interception. Move the dummies farther apart in two-yard intervals until you can determine the distance each backfield candidate can cover effectively.

The better defenders will move with the arm action of the quarterback, they will accelerate faster than others, and will demonstrate extreme competitiveness in their interception attempts. Before very long they will learn to judge rather accurately where the ball is going and get there to intercept it. They learn to get the "jump" on the ball just as a good outfielder in baseball learns to get the jump on a ball. After a while, have the passer fake the ball in one direction and throw it in another. The boy with good pass defense potential will soon learn to recognize fakes and not be deceived into making false moves.

I feel that if a boy cannot perform well in these drills, he will not be an adequate deep zone pass defender. After 15 minutes of these drills each day for one week, a boy should show his potential. If he demonstrates little improvement, is still slow getting started, falls down occasionally, and cannot stay on the line as he moves back, it is time to start looking for some other defensive position for him to play. I believe in that old adage about a sow's ear and a silk purse. Don't try to make a pass defender out of a boy who doesn't have the physical capacity to develop the technique *in the time you have to teach him.*

The best candidates for the three deep positions are usually sprinters and hurdlers who have some basketball experience. Speed is important, yet almost any team has the relative speed to provide *adequate* zone pass defense. Equally important is the development of the player's coordination, reaction time, feel for the ball, and aggressiveness. If one can locate the fast boy who already has these abilities well developed through other sports participation, then the job will be much easier. If one can find three boys with *exceptional* speed, good height, sharp reaction, and smooth coordination, the day is not too distant when you can sit back, relax, and enjoy the game when your team goes on defense.

PLAYING THE THREE DEEP ZONES

Stance

Just prior to the snap of the ball all three deep defenders must assume a "set" position from which they can react with maximum speed. The feet should be spread a comfortable distance, knees bent, hips dropped, arms bent at the elbows and down in front of the body in a relaxed and ready manner. In other words, they should set themselves closer to the ground ready to move in any direction. The feet should have a toe-to-heel stagger and the body weight should be over the ball of the forward foot. The ankles and knees are flexed so that the knees are directly over the toes and all cleats are on the ground. Under no conditions should the defender be permitted to have his hands on his knees or be standing erect when the ball is snapped.

The deep outside defenders should have the outside foot back and the body turned slightly to the outside. This foot and body position provides for the quickest movement in the direction of the deep outside zone. The back's head should be turned in, and by peripheral vision the eyes are watching the quarterback and an assigned key. As a guide, their alignment versus a tight formation would be three to four yards outside a tight end or wingback and six to eight yards off the line of scrimmage (Diagram 5-5).

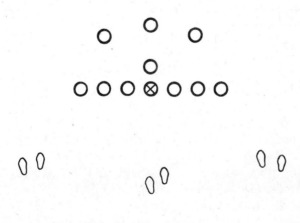

Diagram 5-5

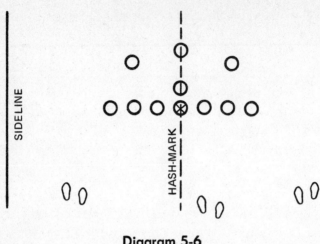

Diagram 5-6

The deep center defender versus a tight balanced formation should have a toe-to-instep relationship of the feet with the body weight slightly forward and the shoulders parallel to the line of scrimmage. The head is facing the ball, and because of his depth, the safety should be able to see the receivers at both ends of the line by using his peripheral vision.

If the football is resting on one of the hash-marks, then the center defender's foot which is toward the open side of the field should be back. From a hash-mark position the safety man on the show of a pass will have to move back at an angle to get into his zone and this foot position facilitates that movement just as it does for the halfbacks (Diagram 5-6).

Keys

The primary responsibility of the three deep defenders is pass defense. However, they are also a vital part of a sound running defense so we can not have them lingering too long in their zones on the *possibility* that a pass may develop. For this reason, these defenders must be assigned positive keys so that within a split-second after the ball has been snapped, they can determine whether the developing play is a pass or run and can react accordingly. I feel that the best keys are those receivers who can get into each of the three deep zones the fastest. Usually this means that the deep outside defenders will key the first eligible receiver in from their sideline. In a "full house" T the safety would key the ball. In an off-set formation he would key the second receiver in

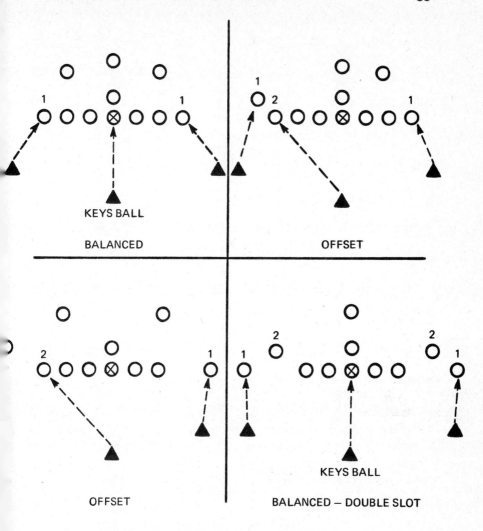

STANDARD KEYS OF THE THREE-DEEP ZONE

Diagram 5-7

from the sideline, and if it were a balanced spread or double slot, he would again key the ball. These become standard keys (Diagram 5-7) and can be used as a starting point for teaching keys and appropriate reactions. Actually, during the season the determination of positive keys becomes a vital part of the preparation for each opponent and, most likely, different keys will be required from week to week as opponents'. offenses change.

Diagram 5-8 illustrates a simple drill for introducing the

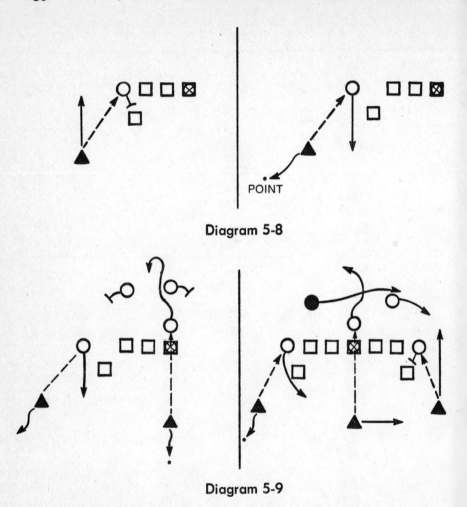

Diagram 5-8

Diagram 5-9

concept of keying. If the end blocks down, the halfback reads "run" and should step forward as if to support the running defense. If the end releases from the line, the halfback looks to the ball while he drop-steps with his outside foot and sprints to his zone ready to play pass defense. The releasing end, of course, may be coming down to block for a running play, but if that were the case, the run would most likely be to the opposite side, so by dropping back on this key our halfback has merely moved into his normal rotation pattern.

The next logical step in developing the key drills is to add a quarterback and a skeleton backfield (Diagram 5-9), then a half-line scrimmage drill (Diagram 5-10), and finally a full rehearsal under game conditions. During the season these drills should be modified

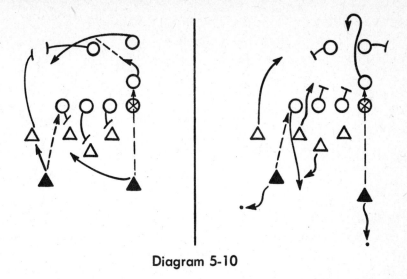

Diagram 5-10

to use the actual keys that will be assigned for a particular opponent.

One of the major problems in teaching keys in a zone defense is to make the boys realize that they are not playing man-for-man pass defense with their key. It is to be emphasized to them that the key is assigned merely to provide a quick "read" as to whether the developing play will be a run or a pass. After they read their key, they should generally disregard this man and react to whatever play action is indicated.

The advantage in assigning as keys those receivers who can most readily release into the various three deep zones is added protection. Since these are the most immediately dangerous receivers, a deep defender will be conscious of each of them on the snap of the ball. In those systems where zone defenders are assigned interior linemen as keys, there is always the possibility that a fast receiver may get the jump on the pass defender while he is concentrating on an ineligible man.

Some coaches prefer not to key on individuals for the proper reactions. Since there is only one ball in a football game, they prefer to have their deep men just concentrate on its whereabouts. "Advantage should be taken of the natural curiosity of a player to look into the backfield." The proponents of this philosophy feel that with proper training it isn't too difficult to recognize the difference between run and pass. But hard-faking backs and fine ball handlers tend to create optical illusions, so to help the deep defenders they are coached to always shuffle back a couple of steps while the illusions clear. The deficiencies of this system are obvious in the delayed reactions that will consequently be made in support of the running defense.

COVERING RECEIVERS IN THE DEEP ZONES

On the show of "pass" the deep defenders retreat immediately to a point near the forward center of their zones from which they can best cover the width of their zone. With the ball in the middle of the field, this means that the two defensive halfbacks will need to move back at an angle toward the sideline to get into the lateral center of their zones. From the stance previously described, outside foot back, these defenders can get a fast start on their "points" by taking a short drop-step with the outside foot, a cross-over with the inside foot, and then sprint to their point while looking back over the shoulder at the quarterback and the ball. This is the same basic running action that was emphasized in the drill in Diagram 5-3, and is similar to a good outfielder's as he goes after a fly ball on a long drive.

The man assigned to the deep center zone will run backwards to his point unless his pre-snap alignment was well off the mid-line of the football field. As he moves back he must be careful to keep his shoulders parallel to the line of scrimmage so he can see both ends of the offensive formation and consequently be aware of receivers coming into his zone from either direction (Diagram 5-11).

Pass defense really begins only after the deep backs have moved to their points. While sprinting back they have been watching the ball and through peripheral vision the development of the pass pattern in their area. Now they will pick up and cover the receiver or receivers in their respective zones.

The deep zone defender must recognize two relationships in the coverage of receivers within his zone: vertical position and lateral position. Vertically he must keep three to five yards deeper than the deepest receiver in his zone. He must keep the receiver in front of him and play him loose. If the receiver gets too close, the defender becomes susceptible to fakes, gets turned in the wrong direction or gets himself in a position where he cannot play the ball when it is thrown. This loss of vertical position is the cardinal sin of pass defense since it involves letting a receiver get behind the pass

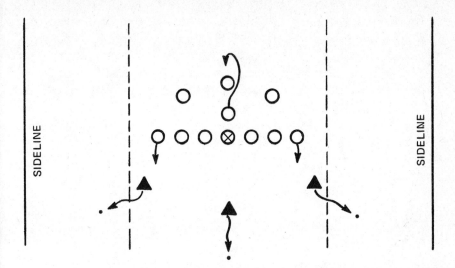

THE DEEP BACKS – MOVEMENT TO POINTS

Diagram 5-11

defender. It is the primary cause of touchdown passes thrown against the zone defense.

As a general rule of lateral position the deep defenders should play the center of their zones until the man-for-man situation develops. As the total pass pattern unfolds, the alert defender can anticipate the most likely receivers to enter his zone and at the critical time favor that side of the zone which will provide a more tight lateral position on him. The deep outside backs should never get closer than six yards to the sideline until the ball is in the air. They should be outside conscious, however, since there is no help to the outside. If no one enters their zone, then they can turn to the inside and help the deep center defender.

The farther back a passer fades and the deeper the receiver runs, the farther the ball must travel in the air to reach the intended receiver. A good pass defender can travel about one-third as fast as a long forward pass in flight, therefore, while a pass travels 30 yards in the air, a defender can move ten yards to intercept it. It follows then that the deeper the patterns the receivers run, the looser the defenders may play in both vertical and lateral position.

With young, inexperienced pass defense candidates it is often advisable to show them the relationship that they should maintain with a receiver by actually jogging or walking them through various routes within the zone. Diagram 5-12 illustrates the movements of the left deep outside zone defender in covering a streak pass, an out pass, and a corner. Notice in all cases that he first sprints to his point, maintains his vertical position, then adjusts his lateral position according to the route of the receiver. After reaching his point, he maintains his vertical position by retreating in the center of his zone. The "stretch drill" gives him confidence that he can intercept any ball thrown in his zone if he stays in the center. Only after the receiver has made his final break does he move laterally with him to achieve an extra advantage.

Pass defenders are often told to "keep the receiver on a line between yourself and the passer." An examination of this old cliché indicates how erroneous it is. In Diagram 5-13, one can readily see that if the defender abides by this maxim, he will be in a vulnerable position in many instances. At position "A" his relationship to the receiver is satisfactory if the ball were to be thrown at that point. However, if the receiver were to break in at that point, the defender would become nothing but a chaser. Likewise in position "B" he would be able to defend the corner pattern, but if the receiver were to break up field he would again be beaten. The position of "C" and "D" are fine relationships, but would be difficult to achieve if the defender had been attempting to apply the maxim throughout the receiver's route. The error in this rule of coverage is that in its application the defender too frequently loses his vertical position. This holds true in covering outside cuts particularly, and as illustrated in "B", leaves the door open for the receiver to get behind the defender. Six points!

The deep zone pass defender must move in such a manner that he is always in control. He must always be watching the passer, but conscious of the receiver's moves. When the receiver changes directions, the defender must turn toward the passer in his change of direction so as not to take his eyes off the ball. The one exception to this rule is when the receiver has beaten him. In that case he must turn and sprint in an effort to regain his vertical position. By watching the receiver's hands and eyes he can determine if the ball has been thrown and at what instant he should turn to attempt the interception.

One of the strengths of a zone defense is the fact that the pass defender should be less susceptible to fakes by the receiver since he is concentrating on the ball and maintaining a loose coverage. Since the curl and sideline patterns are common weapons

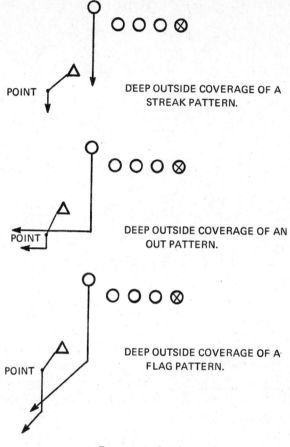

Diagram 5-12

against the zone, the defenders should also be warned against committing themselves on these patterns until the ball is actually in the air. A few completions of these two patterns can sometimes sucker a good defender into moving in on the receiver too early, leaving him open for the "hook and go" or the "sideline and up" patterns.

When no receiver enters a particular deep zone, the defender is free and backs up in his zone in order to assist on any deep pass that may be thrown. He looks particularly for receivers who may be crossing into his zone from an adjacent zone. If there are two receivers in his zone, he maintains his vertical position on the deepest man.

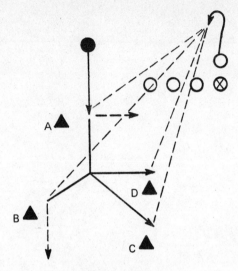

Diagram 5-13

DRILLS FOR COVERING RECEIVERS

In teaching the three deep defenders the techniques of covering receivers in their zones, I have utilized a number of drills which have proven valuable. One is a more realistic version of the stretch drill which is shown in Diagram 5-14. Set the ball on a sideline and have a defender take a position about ten yards deep. Place two receivers on five-yard stripes ten yards apart, and then on the snap of the ball have them release full speed on streak patterns. On the snap of the ball the defender must move back to his point then turn and run to maintain vertical position, staying well ahead of the fastest, deepest man. As the receivers pass the hash mark, the quarterback throws the ball to either receiver, being careful to lead him straight down the yard line. Check the defender to see that he stays in the middle of his zone as he moves back, not favoring one receiver or the other. He should run with his hips facing away from the line of scrimmage, but with his head and shoulders turned so that he can watch the quarterback and the ball. Of course, as soon as the ball is released, he cuts directly to it, attempting an interception if possible. As all defenders become proficient in covering this ten-yard width, move the receivers out to 15 yards and repeat the drill.

The next step in developing individual coverage is illustrated in Diagram 5-15. Here the objective is to give the defender

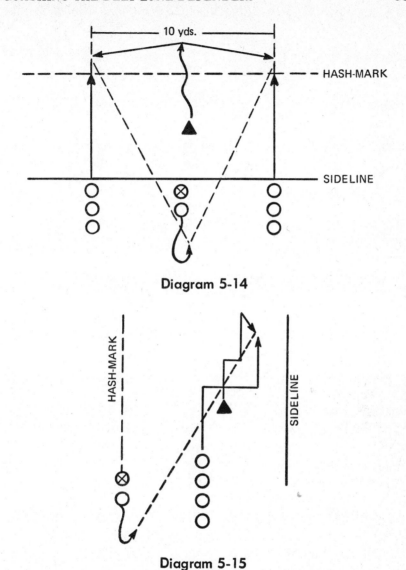

Diagram 5-14

Diagram 5-15

training and experience in covering a single receiver running a variety of patterns within a specific zone. Use the sideline and a hash-mark to define a one-third width of the field and let the receiver run free-lance patterns within this area. Set some type of markers downfield at 15 yards and restrict the receivers from breaking their patterns before reaching these points.

A variation of this drill, which can train a number of men at one time, is illustrated in Diagram 5-16. I have found this drill to be good training for my quarterbacks and receivers too. By having

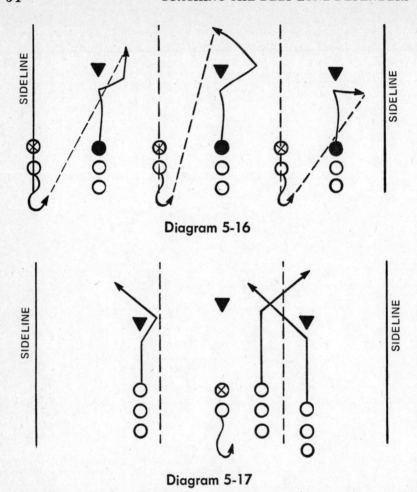

Diagram 5-16

Diagram 5-17

the action in all three zones start at the same time, one can train the quarterbacks in signal cadence, all counting at the same time or each alternately calling signals for all three groups.

To start developing some teamwork between the three deep defenders, the next drill (Diagram 5-17) utilizes three receivers, one in each zone, but they are no longer restricted to staying in their original zones. Rather than having all three free-lance their routes, I prefer to draw up a variety of three-deep patterns from different spread sets which will include deep curls, crossing patterns, overloads, etc. If these are illustrated on 5″ × 7″ cards, a manager can huddle each offensive group and indicate their pattern before they move to the line of scrimmage. With this organization, the drill moves more quickly and the patterns are the type

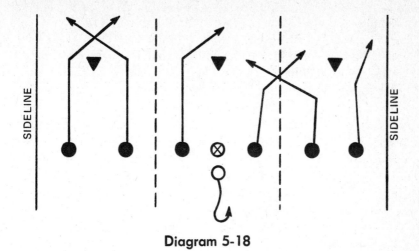

Diagram 5-18

frequently encountered. The defensive coach should emphasize communication between the deep backs, covering the deepest man in a zone, watching the ball, reacting to the ball, and the many other factors previously discussed.

A good confidence drill is presented in the "6 on 3 drill" illustrated in Diagram 5-18. Having successfully defended the deep area in the "3 on 3 drill," the defenders are now exposed to six receivers breaking into their area. Again to coordinate the receivers' routes and avoid the weird patterns that may develop from six men free-lancing, I draw up a half dozen patterns and a manager rotates them to each offensive group running in the drill.

PLAYING THE BALL

Covering or maintaining the proper relationship with the receiver is important but once the ball is in the air, the defensive back must play the ball—never the receiver. If the defender is too receiver-conscious in playing zone pass defense, he will never react at the instant the ball is thrown and will always be one step late. This is the defender who always makes the tackle after the completion, he looks good in this respect, but he seldom breaks up a pass and almost never makes an interception.

He must anticipate when the passer will turn the ball loose. All passers "telegraph" their throws in some manner, so the defenders should study the quarterback, get acquainted with his

movements, his arm action, and even more important his eye action. Regardless of how many receivers may be down field, many
passers have a tendency to watch their primary receivers throughout the development of the play. Many quarterbacks have learned
the art of faking with the ball or faking good arm action, but only
the best have mastered the ability to fake with the head and eyes.

Once the ball leaves the passer's hand all zone defenders
must go to the ball regardless of where they are. This is one of the
strengths of zone defense. Since all defenders are watching the
passer during coverage, they will all be able to react immediately
when the ball is thrown. This simultaneous convergence on the ball
by the entire defensive backfield increases the interception possibilities. The back into whose zone the ball has been thrown
should normally have the greatest opportunity for interception, but
if the ball is poorly thrown or is tipped or batted, the presence of
several defenders in the area increases the chances that one of
them will come up with the ball. The rallying of defensive backs to
the football can serve other purposes too. If an interception is
made, it assures a number of blockers in the immediate vicinity to
spring the ball carrier loose for a good return. The element of
human error is always present in football and if the defensive man
in whose zone the ball has been thrown misjudges the ball, or falls
down, this does not necessarily mean a touchdown for the opponent. The other defenders reacting to the ball may be in position at
least to make the tackle.

Since the opposing passer will be trying to throw the ball
away from the defensive man, the defender will generally have to
change direction in order to play the ball. If he has been moving
backward and the ball is thrown in front or to the left or right of
him, the defender must plant his back foot and drive off in the new
direction. Quick recovery and extra speed in moving to the ball are
vital at this stage. *He must not run in circles* as he reacts to the ball.
He must anticipate his point of interception and drive directly to it.
Play the ball through, over, or in front of the receiver. The defender cannot interfere or push or shove the receiver while the ball is in
the air but he does have an equal right to the ball and he should
play it tough. This concept of equal rights has to be instilled in a
pass defender early in his career. The most important fundamental
in pass defense is the desire to intercept. He must not be intimi-
dated by the presence of the receiver or an official. The ball in the
air is as much his as it is the intended receiver's and he has a right
to go after it. One of the best drills I have used for developing this

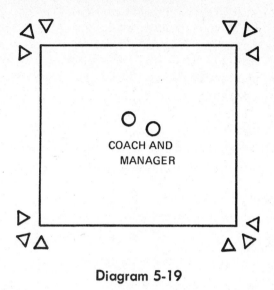

Diagram 5-19

aggressive ball-hawking attitude is illustrated in Diagram 5-19. I had originally used this drill to teach rebounding during my brief career as a basketball coach and later adapted it to football, since the desired objective is the same—get the ball.

Place the defenders in groups of three at each corner of a ten-yard square. The coach stands in the middle of the square and tosses a football into the air in such a manner that it will come down in the middle of one group, then the next, working around the square in a clockwise direction. Each of the three players in each group attempts to catch the ball without illegally interfering with the other two. Emphasize proper timing in leaping for the ball as well as the use of the hips to screen or block out an opponent or to protect one's own position.

By using three balls and having a manager standing beside him to catch the return of the balls, a coach can give 12 defensive backs a lot of experience in this drill in three minutes. After the players have become familiar with the drill, I stimulate more aggressiveness by requiring the two unsuccessful defenders in each group to sprint around the square and be set up again before their next turn is due.

Finally, I move the groups out so that they are 20 yards apart and then loft high passes beyond each group and to their left and right. Now they are fighting for interceptions on the run, more like game conditions, whereas in the first phase of the drill they were merely "rebounding."

It is difficult for the deep defender to play the ball on well thrown hook passes and sideline passes without interfering with the receiver. As these patterns develop, the zone defender must still maintain his vertical distance until the ball is thrown, then if it appears he will be screened from playing the ball by the receiver's body, he should run a collision course with the receiver, timing himself to arrive at the same time as the ball. If the ball is thrown low at waist level as it should be, he has no recourse but to ram the receiver with a jarring shoulder tackle hoping to make him cough up the ball. On the other hand if it is coming in above the waist, the defender should drive into the receiver high, while pulling down on his arms, stripping him of the ball.

COORDINATING THE THREE DEEP DEFENDERS

The three deep defenders must work together as a unit assisting and supporting each other. Communication is vital and they should be encouraged to talk to each other during the development of a play, alerting each other to potential receivers leaving one area and going into another. They should call out loud and clear, "take him" or "man across." Linebackers also are helped tremendously when the three deep men alert them to what is happening, so for their benefit, too, the deep backs should be constantly calling the action. Linebackers cannot see what is happening behind them and even their vision in front is sometimes obscured, so such calls as "draw," "screen," "curl in," or "curl out" are most helpful to them.

One man, preferably the center safety, should be designated as responsible for coordinating variations in the play of the three deep men. Particularly, he should check the lateral alignment of the unit. With the ball resting in the middle of the field, these men can align themselves with respect to the ball, however, if the ball is resting on a hashmark, the deep backs cannot align on the ball but must adjust to the open side of the field. I have stated that the three deep men each must be capable of covering a lateral distance of 17⅔ yards, but they are seldom called upon to do this. The extremities of the outside zones are rarely threatened by deep passes except on the short side when the ball is on or near a hash-mark. Look at it this way. If the ball is on the right hash-mark and the quarterback were to throw a pass 20 yards deep to a re-

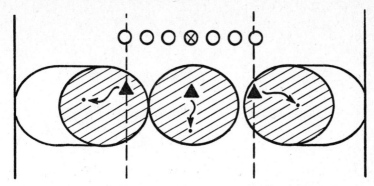

A. BALL IN CENTER OF FIELD. TIGHT FORMATION.

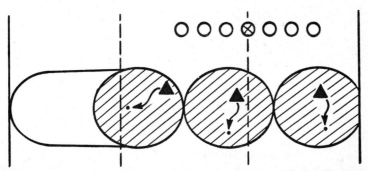

B. BALL AT RIGHT HASH-MARK. TIGHT FORMATION.

Diagram 5-20

ceiver near the opposite sideline, the ball would have to travel laterally about 35 yards making it a poor investment. The ball would hang in the air too long making it vulnerable to an interception which in turn would probably result in a touchdown since the bulk of the offensive team would be on the opposite side of the field.

In reality then, the zones that the three deep men will cover are less than the theoretical 17⅔ yards (Diagram 5-20). The center zone will initially be the smallest in width as the outside defenders drop back to their zone points. Nor will these points be in the center of their assigned one-third of the field as previously stated, but rather in the center of that portion of the deep outside area into which a receiver may logically break. As the total pass pattern develops, however, a receiver moving farther to the deep outside

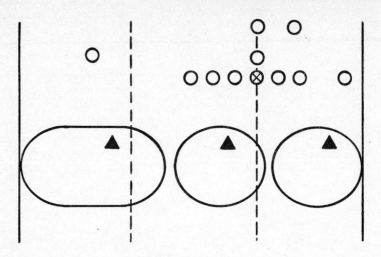

Diagram 5-21

may require that defender to adjust his lateral position farther to the outside. As this is done, the center defender must maintain his relationship by loosening up to that side also and assuming a larger width of responsibility. If all receivers continued on deep routes, eventually the three deep defenders would arrive at that theoretical situation in which they would each be covering one third of the field and maintaining a point in the lateral center of that zone. This is highly unlikely, of course, because such a pass pattern is unfeasible in the first place and second, the pass rush should certainly deny the development of a pattern that would require this much time.

The use of split receivers will require adjustments of the three deep defenders before the ball is snapped, and here again the center safety should be alert to maintaining their proper relationship (Diagram 5-21). Even under these circumstances it is not necessary or advisable for the deep men to move initially to points in the center of their theoretical zones. As a general rule, the wider a receiver splits, the farther inside of him the defender can initially play and still provide adequate coverage so long as he maintains his vertical distance.

The variety of adjustments in the lateral relationship of the three deep men are infinite and therefore must be narrowed down in preparation for the specific offensive sets and pass patterns of each opponent. These adjustments should always be practiced and rehearsed on a marked practice field so that the players have the reference points of yard line, sidelines, and hash-marks to guide them in attaining and maintaining proper alignment. Walk them through the adjustments of position that are necessary for each offensive set as the ball is moved from hash-mark to hash-mark, then review the opponent's favorite pass patterns. Regardless of the offensive set or position of the ball on the field, the three deep defenders should never be more than 15 yards apart nor closer together than ten yards as they take their pre-snap positions. These relative positions should be maintained as they drop back to their initial zone points, and are held until the receivers make their final breaks and the man-for-man situation develops.

Chapter 6

DEFENDING THE

SHORT PASSING ZONE

The first rule of pass defense is to avoid the long touchdown pass, and to that end a great amount of effort must be expended in increasing the effectiveness of the deep defenders. The short zones, however, can easily become the Achilles' heel of an otherwise efficient pass defense unit. Many fine pass offenses today are predicated on ball control—not the "bomb"—and their primary target areas are the short zones. Many coaches who were formerly advocates of the "three yards and a cloud of dust" style of offense are now advocates of a "three passes and a first down" philosophy. Then, too we have all had teams that suffered from the "third down syndrome." After being held to four or five yards in two plays, the opposing quarterback would consistently and inevitably drill a third-down pass into the arms of an open receiver breaking into one of the short zones, to keep their drive alive.

The only solution to these frustrations is hard work. The same amount of time that is devoted to training the deep zone defenders must be allocated to training the short zone defenders. But we are generally reluctant to do this. Coaches will drill inside linebackers by the hour to make them proficient in plugging holes in the running defense, and yet some of the key plays in any ball game are the short passes thrown into the linebacker zones.

There are four short zones, but we cannot consider them as similar. In most defensive schemes, the two inside zones will be covered by inside linebackers, while the two flat zones will generally be covered by outside backers, defensive ends, or deep backs moving up on rotations or secondary stunts (Diagram 6-1).

102

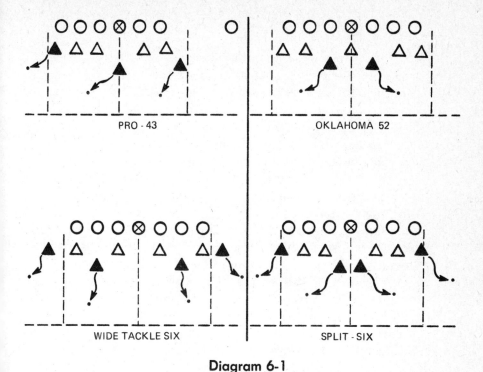

Diagram 6-1

The inside zones are much smaller in lateral dimensions than the flat zones. They extend from the line of scrimmage to a depth of 10 to 12 yards. The flat zones likewise extend to a 10- to 12-yard depth, but must also include the swing pass area behind the line of scrimmage, making them larger in both dimensions.

COVERING THE INSIDE ZONES

Since the manner in which the inside linebackers play in zone coverage is so vastly different from that of the deep defenders or the flat defenders, it is necessary to consider them separately. Much of this variance in technique is a result of the fact that the inside linebackers' first responsibility is defense against the running game. This places him closer to the line of scrimmage and usually well inside the lateral position of most eligible receivers.

Even the linebacker's stance must be dictated by the requirements of the running defense. His concern in stance is primarily related to being able to meet and react to blockers, not pass receivers.

The lateral position of the linebacker is determined by the team defensive alignment that has been called, but he, himself, determines his vertical position. He must anticipate the type of offensive play that will be called and take his depth accordingly. Normally, on short yardage situations he will play closer to the line of scrimmage, while on pass situations he may drop off slightly or move back just prior to the snap of the ball.

Keys are as essential to the inside linebackers as they are to the deep defenders. However, a linebacker's key will generally be an interior lineman or one of the running backs. As his key indicates pass, the linebacker drops to his point within the short zone which is his responsibility in the team scheme of defense for that particular play. Just as the deep defenders, he too watches the quarterback and the ball as he moves to his point. The quarterback's drop-back technique may provide a tip-off as to the type of pass play developing. If he backs out from the center, a quick pass to a receiver breaking into one of the short zones can be expected and the linebacker must be ready to react immediately. On the other hand, if the quarterback uses the traditional drop-step, cross-over, and retreat, the pass will be deeper or at least more delayed in its development.

There is considerable controversy among pass defense coaches as to the best method for linebackers to move to their initial points. Some teach the "drop-step and cross-over" and others advocate the "back up, keep your shoulders squared" technique. I feel that if the backer is already aligned laterally in the defensive formation so that he is approximately in the center of his zone of responsibility, then he should merely run backwards to get to the back of his zone. This technique has the advantage of allowing him good peripheral vision left and right as he moves to his point. But if he must move laterally to get to the center of his assigned zone and consequently his point, then speed is more important than peripheral vision in both directions so he should drop-step to the side of his move, cross-over and sprint at top speed gaining depth as he moves out. In a play-action pass, this same technique is advisable even though the linebacker may be initially in the center of his zone. He will have had to delay momentarily while he checked the run threat so now he must get depth as quickly as possible and the drop-step, cross-over technique is fastest for most people.

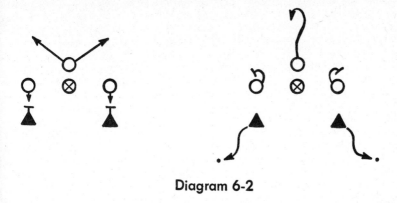

Diagram 6-2

One of the early drills for training inside linebackers must be the keying drill illustrated in Diagram 6-2. In this drill the backer has been assigned an interior lineman as his key. If the lineman drives out toward him, the backer steps in to meet him, using blocker protection techniques, ready to shed him and react appropriately to a running play. If the lineman drops back in a passer protection position, the inside linebacker retreats quickly to a point within his zone.

Training the deep backs requires many sessions devoted to extending their capacity to cover lateral distances. The same requirement holds true in the development of linebackers. They, too, have an assigned pass coverage zone which has a specific lateral distance and they must be capable of covering it. A good drill for "stretching" the linebacker's capacity for lateral coverage is shown in Diagram 6-3. As the quarterback drops back, the linebacker retreats to the rear center of his zone while watching the quarterback. He must be in control and ready to react instantly to the arm action of the quarterback. As the quarterback sets, he throws to one of the stationary receivers beyond the rear limits and just outside the linebacker's zone. The linebacker, of course, plays the ball in front of the receiver attempting to intercept. After attaining his point, the linebacker should break directly left or right, parallel to the line of scrimmage as he moves on his interception route. He must be careful not to drift deeper in his route nor to run a curved path to the ball.

The inside linebacker who is capable of getting rapidly to his proper position, then covering a good lateral distance, assists the pass rush as well as the pass coverage. His position in front of a receiver will force the quarterback to delay his throw until the

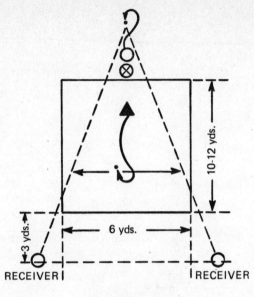

Diagram 6-3

receiver clears the linebacker. This delay may be adequate for the pass rush to effectively interfere with the passer.

COVERING THE RECEIVER IN THE INSIDE ZONES

The inside linebacker in zone pass defense has two responsibilities—coverage of a man in his assigned zone and providing in-front coverage of men in the deep zones. The techniques that he uses in carrying out these responsibilities are vastly different from the techniques employed by other zone defenders. This is a point frequently overlooked by coaches who merely include their linebackers in the pass defense drills of the deep backs.

In covering a receiver in an inside zone, a major problem is the quickness with which the receiver can enter the zone. If a tight receiver is uncovered, he poses a constant threat to the inside short zones, so it is for this reason that most sound defenses today position a lineman or linebacker on the tight receiver to delay him or to deny him certain routes. A coach would like his inside backers to have at least time enough to get into position in the rear of their zones. This is not always possible, of course, so the backer must be prepared to react even while he moves into position. If he is assigned the additional responsibility for delaying or denying a tight receiver, then he may have to fight the receiver all the way as he moves to his zone point.

The linebacker's pass defense techniques are much more physical than the deep backs'. At every opportunity he should push, bump, and shove receivers as they attempt to execute their patterns. He can do this because he has no deep responsibility. He does not have to concern himself about the receiver getting behind him.

A cardinal rule of the inside zones is that the linebackers *never* allow a receiver to run a route in front of them unmolested. Whether the defender is still retreating to the rear of his zone or has already gained his position, on the show of a receiver cutting across between himself and the line of scrimmage, the backer should step forward and into him delivering a solid rip or shiver to knock him down or to at least destroy the timing of the pattern. This is the best weapon the linebacker has for short passes just over the line of scrimmage, and it also denies drag patterns and floods in which a tight end attempts to move to the opposite side by running a shallow route in front of the linebackers.

The receiver who attempts patterns which route him into the inside zones should be made to pay the price. The linebackers should be most aggressive in handling him, not only to destroy the pattern he is currently running, but also to make him wary and more concerned about his personal welfare than reception of the ball.

Passes in this area are directed to the chest level and receivers are taught to turn their numbers in toward the passer making it almost an impossibility to intercept. If the ball is in flight before physical contact can be made with the receiver, then the linebacker must time himself to effect a collision course arriving at the instant the receiver touches the ball. Contact should be made with the shoulder directed to the back of the chest area and the arms should drive down hard over the arms of the receiver stripping him from top to bottom.

Since few defenses today allow tight receivers to fly off the line of scrimmage, the hook pass is now less of a threat to the inside linebacker zones than it was several years ago. We still refer to the short zone directly in front of a tight end position as the "hook zone," but the pass threat in this area today is largely from split receivers and halfbacks running curl-in and slant-in patterns. If the slant-in pattern is being thrown to a receiver who is split more than five yards, the target area is too far outside the inside backer in most defenses for him to be effective in preventing it. However, if the inside backer is watching the quarterback and the ball as he retreats to his zone point, he will be in ideal position to "lower the boom" on the receiver the instant after he catches the ball, frequently producing a fumble. His depth at the moment the ball is thrown should put him in the direct path of the receiver and his reaction to the ball as it is thrown should have turned him toward the receiver on a collision course. His own aggressiveness will now determine whether or not a fumble can be produced (Diagram 6-4).

Curl-in patterns are run into areas which are uncovered by the inside linebackers. The trend today is to run them deeper, breaking at 12-14 yards and coming back into the rear of the inside short zones or into the seams. They are especially effective to take advantage of stunting linebackers who have left an inside zone vacant. The initial leg of the pattern drives the deep zone defender back in his area of responsibility, then the curl is made into a vacant short zone or between two short zone protectors (Diagram 6-5).

The inside backer must defend the curl by playing in front of it as he would on other deep routes, getting his depth in the zone, then reading the quarterback's actions and reacting laterally to the ball as it is thrown.

The linebacker on the tight end side of an offensive set should anticipate a curl-in by the split back on this side whenever the tight end releases quickly into the flat. As he drops to his zone point, the linebacker should always check the tight end by peripheral vision since he is the receiver who can most quickly get into his zone. If the end breaks out, the linebacker should move to a position further out from his usual zone point and expect the split receiver to curl-in behind him (Diagram 6-6).

ASSISTING THE COVERAGE OF THE DEEP ZONES

Bear in mind that the standard zone defensive scheme has two bands of defenders: those protecting the short zones and those protecting the deep zones. The primary responsibility of the short zone defenders is to prevent the completion of passes in their zones. However, they have a secondary responsibility to assist in the coverage of deep zone receivers by playing in front of them,

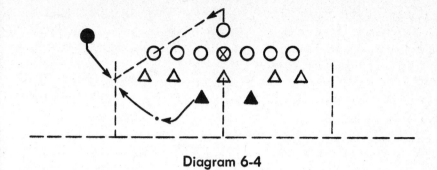

Diagram 6-4

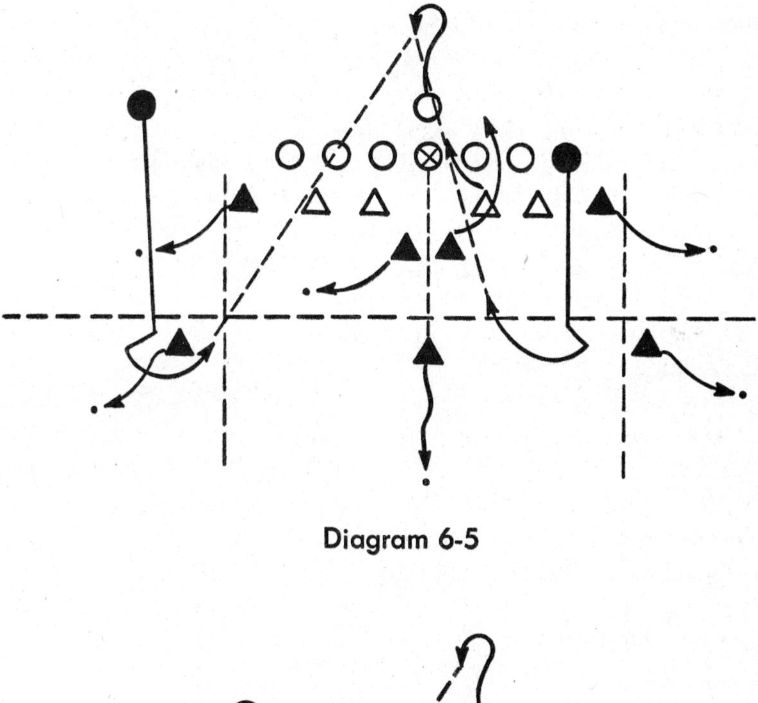

Diagram 6-5

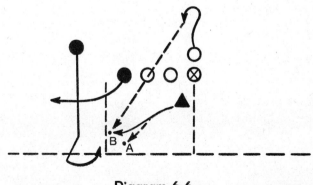

Diagram 6-6

denying certain patterns, obscuring the quarterback's vision, providing interception possibilities, forcing the quarterback to loft the ball to his deep receivers, and delaying the development of many patterns.

The old pass defense axiom, "don't let the receiver get behind you", does not apply to the short zone defenders. The linebacker moves to his zone point, bumping and shoving receivers going through his zone if the opportunity presents itself, but at 10-12 yards depth he levels off and checks the receiver on a deep route into the deep zone defender. Playing for the interception and harassing the quarterback and receiver are now his objectives.

Diagram 6-7 illustrates a good drill to train the inside backer in how to drop to his zone point, square off, read the quarterback's eyes and arm movements, and play the ball in front of a deep receiver who is maneuvering behind him.

Since the interceptions a linebacker may make in front of deep receivers are frequently line-drive type passes, the drill in Diagram 6-8 provides experience in catching this type of pass. A few minutes experience in these two drills each day will pay big dividends in increased proficiency of the inside linebackers.

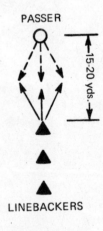

Diagram 6-8

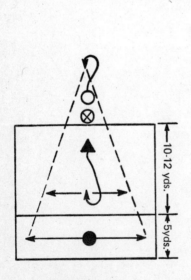

Diagram 6-7

COVERING THE FLAT ZONES

Covering the flat zones presents some special problems in pass defense. One aspect is the peculiar nature of the flat zone, particularly its rectangular dimensions whose width varies from about 9 to 26 yards depending upon the lateral position of the ball on the field. This makes the flat zone a difficult area to defend merely from the standpoint of width. However, another problem is presented by the depth of the zone. Unlike the inside zones, the flats must include that area *behind* the line of scrimmage in which swing passes and screen passes are so frequently thrown. Although the flat zone defender will not normally move across the line of scrimmage to pass protect in this area, he must, nevertheless, be responsible for receivers in that area.

Several factors assist the man assigned zone responsibility for flat coverage. Drop-back passes thrown in the flat area beyond the line of scrimmage are necessarily long passes and consequently the defender has more time to react to the ball than defenders of the inside zones. Then too, flat passes are dangerous passes and an interception in this area can result in a long return or possible touchdown. Finally, the proficiency of most passers throwing into the flats is not as great as it is throwing to the short inside zones or downfield. With the exception of the sideline pattern, most drop-back type passers neglect their practice of flat passes. The next time you watch a team in pre-game warm-up note how few flat zone type patterns are thrown by the quarterbacks—flares, hitches, swing and screen passes, slants, square outs, and the quick break-in or break-out patterns of split receivers. Most quarterbacks like the flag and post patterns, the hooks, curls, and streaks and, given a ball and a receiver, this is what they will throw, always working downfield, seldom throwing flat patterns. The flat is a different dimension. Here they are throwing as much or more to the sideline as downfield. The perspective is different and the angles and leads are different, but these facts are seldom appreciated by quarterbacks, and so, few of them develop a real proficiency in this phase of the passing game.

Those defenders assigned to the flats are a different breed from those playing the inside zones. The size of the zone implies a greater need for speed, and the more open style of play at the flank permits a sacrifice of size if necessary. The flat zone protectors are akin to the deep zone defenders and in many defenses will, in fact, rotate back to a deep zone responsibility in certain adjustments.

The pre-snap position of the flat zone protector is vital to good coverage, and since many coaches also assign outside running responsibility to this man, he must set up in his zone to accomplish both objectives. He must be wide enough to cover the widest receiver threatening his zone, yet he must not be so removed from the next defender to his inside that they cannot mutually support each other against the running attack.

Four common methods of providing flat coverage against a tight formation are illustrated in Diagram 6-9.

Whatever method is used, the cardinal rule of first gaining depth in the zone continues to hold true. On reading drop-back pass, the defender must retreat to a zone point from which he can observe the receivers threatening his zone and react accordingly. Of course in the invert, the back is observing potential receivers and adjusting his depth as he moves into the flat zone. In contrast to covering the inside zones it is not necessary that the flat defender's zone point be in the rear center of the zone. Against tight formations where the receiver must come from the inside, the defender should attain a zone point wide enough to assure maintenance of an initial outside position on the potential receiver.

To cover split receivers adequately in the flat zone it is necessary to adjust the defensive alignment. Unless the split receiver is assigned on a straight man-to-man basis to another back, the flat defender can protect his zone only by moving out on the split man. The coach should provide his defender with definite split rules to apply during the game. For example, if a monster man is playing the zone, one might give him the following guidance: play outside the split man to three yards; from 3-5 yards, play head-up on him; beyond five yards play inside of him but drop off the zone sufficiently to be able to watch the split receiver and quarterback with peripheral vision. Do not take a position closer than five yards from the sideline. If the receiver lines up near the sideline, he has restricted himself to streak patterns and cuts to the inside.

If two receivers come into the flat zone, the defender applies the usual zone pass defense rule of covering the deeper man. Because of the sometime extreme width of his zone, however, the flat protector may also be faced with the problem of two receivers at the same depth, but spaced laterally. In such case, he

SPLIT 6: ENDS DROPPING OFF TO FLAT ZONES

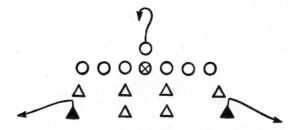

44 STACK: OUTSIDE LINEBACKERS COVERING FLAT ZONES

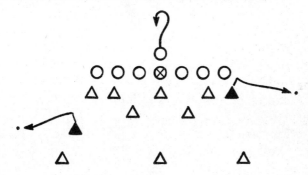

OKLAHOMA 52: MONSTER AND WEAK-SIDE END COVERING FLAT ZONES

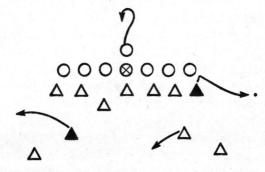

OKLAHOMA 52: INVERT BACK AND ADJUSTED 1 LB COVERING FLAT ZONES

Diagram 6-9

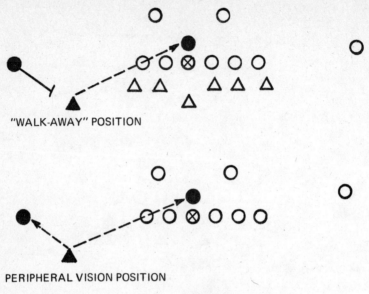

"WALK-AWAY" POSITION

PERIPHERAL VISION POSITION

Diagram 6-10

must maintain a position to assure coverage of the widest receiver. He should be able to expect help if a completion is made to the inside man, but if the pass is successful to the wide man, a breakaway is possible.

Caution most be maintained in taking positions on split receivers, particularly when the defender also has outside running responsibility. Visual contact should always be maintained on the split man to avoid the crack-back block. This negates the position which is frequently referred to as the "walk-away" position— midway between the split man and the next offensive player to his inside (Diagram 6-10). Attaining peripheral vision of the quarterback and the wide split receiver requires the defender to play closer to the receiver and 5-6 yards off the line of scrimmage. This extra vertical distance from the receiver is possible because of his distance from the quarterback. The further the receiver splits, the deeper the defender can set up in his zone.

Another successful technique of playing the wide split receiver is "helmet inside" on the line of scrimmage. From this position the defender should step out and into the receiver giving him a substantial rip with the outside forearm at the line of scrimmage, forcing him to release to the outside. This contact must be accomplished "blind" since the defender must watch the quarter-back and the ball. Immediately, the pass defender must drop back in his zone, "feeling" the receiver as he does so. His inside position denies throwing to this man and also prevents him from breaking in. After carrying the split man to the rear limits of the flat zone, he can check him off to the back having deep outside responsibility, then shift inside to a zone point from which he can continue to cover his zone against other threats.

Swing passes and outside screen passes can cause some concern on the part of the flat zone defender. These might be classified as a type of flood pattern since in most cases a decoy receiver has been sent into or through the zone to draw that defender away from the intended receiver. If the flat zone defender has taken a proper pre-snap lateral position and then moved in depth to a zone point from which he can observe his area and the quarterback, he should have no trouble seeing the screen pass develop. As he recognizes it, he should square laterally with the receiver and slide out with him, but not cross the line of scrimmage until the ball is thrown. As he moves into a swing pass receiver he should maintain outside leverage, tackling with the inside shoulder, head to the outside, denying any possibility of escape to the outside. If a screen pass is being executed, he may have little opportunity to tackle the receiver and may have to be content with jamming the interference. Again, if there is considerable distance to the sideline, he should maintain an outside leverage hoping at worst to force the receiver to the inside where help should be available.

UNIT COORDINATION

Generally, in discussing coverage of the short zones I have disregarded offensive formations and field position. Naturally, these factors are of prime importance in pass defense but must be considered in the whole rather than in the parts. The adjustments and movements that the short zone defenders make to assist each other in the total defensive scheme must be well coordinated, planned in advance, and rehearsed in practice.

To accommodate the pass defense, very little adjustment of the lateral position of the inside zone defenders based upon field position is possible in most defenses. The running threats that must

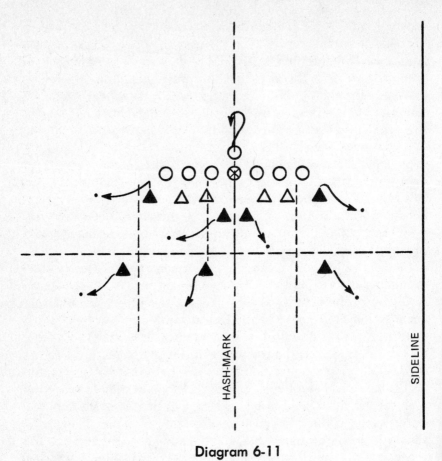

Diagram 6-11

be anticipated by these players necessarily restricts their pre-snap positions. On the show of "pass," however, these men like all other pass defenders can adjust their zones as they move to their zone points. (Diagram 6-11). By sliding the inside zones to the open side of the field from a harsh-mark we can reduce the area of the open field flat zone and also continue to provide in-front assistance to the deep zone defenders who are likewise adjusting to the open side. As we have seen in Chapter 5, the deep zone defenders can make some pre-shap adjustment of their zones by sliding from the hash-mark to the open side, but their primary responsibility is pass defense. Too, their responsibility to support the running defense is primarily on the flanks, so they also strengthen that capacity by sliding to the open side, the more vulnerable flank.

      This concept of sliding zones left and right, depending upon the lateral position of the ball on the field, is another coaching point which should be illustrated to the team on the blackboard and, if necessary, lined out on the practice field. We as coaches, because of our experience, too frequently assume that the young football player understands seemingly basic principles such as this and fail to emphasize the details necessary for complete comprehension. When he fails to perform properly in game conditions, we wonder why. All of the pass defenders must have the *same* mental picture of how the zones slide to the open side and where their new boundaries are if the team effort is to be coordinated.

The offensive formation will be another factor modifying the adjustment of zones. If the offensive pass potential has been set predominantly into the sideline from a hash-mark ball position, it is possible that the defensive team would not want to slide the pass zones to the open field.

A thorough analysis of the scouting reports of an opponent must be made to determine a set of guidelines for the zone pass defenders. One must refer back to an opponent's formation tendencies, down and distance, and field position tendencies to establish when, and when not, to slide the zones. These determinations must be arrived at from a thorough study of the opponent and they should not be left to guesswork. It is the coaching staff's responsibility to provide the defensive captains with positive guideliines for adjustment of the defense with respect to both field position and offensive formations.

Finally, a word must be said about the zone defenders who are "free," the men who do not have receivers in their zones. The short zone protectors should move to their defensive points checking for potential receivers as they move. If on arrival no receivers are in their area or threatening their area, they should give ground, gain greater depth, and widen out in their zone. They must watch the quarterback and the ball, attempting to get between the quarterback and deep receivers downfield. They must not leave their zone unless they are certain that no delayed receivers will enter, and like all other zone defenders, they must react to the ball when it is thrown.

The short zone defenders are vital to good zone pass defense. Without them, an average passer throwing under the deep defenders can destroy the defensive effort. As with the deep defenders, sufficient practice time must be allocated to this phase of pass defense and the personnel provided with sufficient training to develop the mental and physical skills that are essential to this phase of the game.

Chapter 7

UTILIZING THE

THREE-DEEP ZONE

In the construction of a workable pass defense there are two elements that must receive attention. The first embodies the teaching and learning of the individual skills by the players. The second is the forging of the team scheme of pass defense. In Chapters 5 and 6, the principles and mechanics of playing the deep zones were presented.

In reference to specific zones, rather than to specific zone defenses, as stated previously, I want to avoid the tendency to expound a particular pass defense or defensive system. It would be inappropriate, however, to avoid completely an examination of team defenses for we need to appreciate the application of principles and skills in the contexts in which they may be utilized.

Chapter 2 listed a number of advantages of zone pass defense; probably most significant is the strength of the zone against deep passes. I believe this is the key factor in the current trend of adoption of the zone by many professional teams. But one considering this type of defense must be willing to sacrifice a percentage of completions to stop the long ones. Generally, more passes will be completed but few of these will be of the deep variety. The zone team will frequently give up a short flat zone and passes will be completed in front of and between the linebackers and flat zone protectors—but even the passes thrown in these areas must be perfect. An outstanding passer will be able to achieve the short passes, but if he throws too hard or too soft, or over the receiver's head, then the zone defense is in an advantageous position for an interception.

118

Defense in depth is one of the requirements of any sound team defense and most exponents of the zone feel that this system best exemplifies it. Its very nature requires bands of defenders at different depths preventing a quick break-through at any point. Whether the defense is a two-deep, three-deep, or a four-deep alignment, there are always at least three levels or bands that must be penetrated in a zone defense—the line, the short zones, and the deep zones—assuring good strength against the running attack as well as the pass. We shall in the next two chapters examine the nature of the basic types of zone defense, three-and four-deep alignments, but before getting into those details, it may be well to acquaint the reader with a few important drills that can be adapted to any zone alignment.

TEAM DRILLS

Whether one is drilling individuals, units, or the entire team in pass defense, it is absolutely essential that this work be done on a properly lined field complete with hash-marks. So much of this phase of the game is related to distance relationships that the five-yard stripes, the hash-marks, and the sidelines should be present as constant reference points and guidelines.

One of the first drills for the entire pass defense backfield working together should be the "drop to points" drill illustrated in Diagram 7-1. Assuming the opponent is in a balanced tight offensive alignment, set the drill in the middle of the field and on the 50 yard line. As the quarterback steps under the center, all defenders should assume their pre-snap positions and stances, coaches should check for proper alignment, correct body position, proper foot placement—all players should be watching the quarterback. As the quarterback drops to his cup, all defenders should retreat to their initial zone points and square up, ready to defend their zones.

Have they dropped back the desired distance? Did anyone take his eyes off the quarterback? Do they have the proper lateral and vertical distance between each other?

Move the offensive set to one of the hash-marks now and point out the adjustment of zones that you desire to the open field. At this stage of training it is best to confine your coaching to the same simple balanced offensive set—do not attempt to teach adjustment to field position and adjustment to a variety of offensive

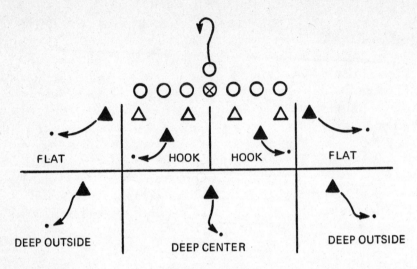

Diagram 7-1

sets at the same time. First things first. There is always the one
player who grasps things immediately and asks the inevitable, "But
what if. . ., Coach?" Shut him off gently while you make sure
everyone understands the *simplest* adjustment first. In coaching,
always teach to the dumbest player, for if you have to play him and
he does not understand his assignment, he will lose ball games for
you.

  I cannot over-emphasize the importance of practicing adjustment of zones to field position. An offensive team will rarely be
in the center of the field more than ten times during a football
game, which implies that some adjustment, however slight, should
be made to meet the other 40 to 50 locations that the offensive
team will have from hash-mark to hash-mark.

  When satisfied with the defenders' movement to zone, the
next phase in the development of teamwork is to have the quarterback throw the ball. Have him lob the ball into various areas of the
defense while again checking their reactions, concentration on the
ball, and movement to the ball.

  The routes various defenders take in moving to the ball are
similar to those they would take in pursuit of a running play. If they
are in the general vicinity of the intended receiver, the defenders
should sprint to the target area taking an interception route if that
opportunity presents itself. Those defenders who are some distance from the receiver should take a route which will assure a

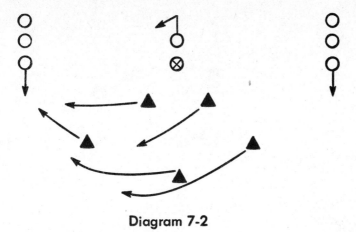

Diagram 7-2

proper angle to tackle the receiver if the pass is completed. Diagram 7-2 illustrates a pass pursuit drill. The passer should fake and then throw to a receiver. The defenders sprint to the ball taking proper pursuit angle to make a two-handed touch tackle. Place the receivers two yards in from the sidelines.

As mentioned earlier, the zone defenses provide better opportunities for interceptions than the man-for-man defense. If the defenders are keying the ball as they should be and pursuing properly, a number of them will be in the vicinity of the ball when it is thrown, consequently if an interception is made, a number of defensive men will be available to pick up blocks which in turn will enhance the possibilities of a sizable return. Diagram 7-3 illustrates a good intercept-block drill which develops this "block response."

Set four dummies as indicated and at a depth of ten yards. As the quarterback retreats, all defenders should move to their points. As the quarterback throws the ball, all of the backs should take a proper pursuit angle to the ball, then block away from the interceptor on the nearest dummy.

Most of the tackles made on interceptions are made by the intended receiver so the next defensive man arriving in the area must block this man. When this player is eliminated, the chances of a long run back are greatly increased.

Finally, all of the above coaching points can be combined in the "skeletal cut game" drill.

Set up a skeleton offensive unit versus a full defensive backfield. The offensive unit can use any cuts or patterns that they wish. Place the ball on the 50 yard line and allow three downs to

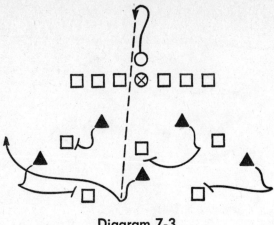

Diagram 7-3

make a first and ten. Award six points for a touchdown scored by the offense or defense, but require the defense to return the ball only to the 50 yard line. Return the ball to the 50 yard line whenever the offense fails to make a first down. Require the quarterbacks to deliver the ball in 3.5 seconds. This drill provides game-like conditions for the defensive backfield while the coaching staff can observe and check all aspects of their play. By establishing a scoring system the motivation of competition can stimulate interest and greater effort.

TYPICAL THREE-DEEP ZONE

Whether one eventually decides to use a two-deep, three-deep, or four-deep zone defense, it must be recognized that the *basic* zone defense is a three-deep alignment. The two-deep zone is a specialty type defense while many of the coverages of the four deep-zone actually develop into a three-man coverage as we shall see in Chapter 8.

Many coaches share a philosophy of zone defense which is "never change the deep defense." To their way of thinking the traditional three-deep zone is the best pass defense, providing the greatest insurance against the long touchdown. By placing three men in these deep positions and leaving them there, training them constantly in protecting their zones and working together as a unit, these coaches develop proficiency in this phase of defense. Any changes in the defensive scheme must come in the use of linebackers or linemen or by changing the rush. If eight men rush, the intermediate defense is sacrificed. If three men rush, the rushing game has been sacrificed to get better short and intermediate coverage. The three-deep coverage is never sacrificed.

Diagram 7-1 illustrates a simple three-deep defense with a six-man front. From a pass defense point of view, this defense gives the best possible coverage of all zones while leaving four men to rush the passer. It is also a defense that offers the simplest adjustments to all offensive formations.

The halfbacks versus a tight formation line up six to eight yards deep and two to three yards outside the offensive ends. They look through the offensive ends to the quarterback and key the ends for the pass-run indication. When the ends show "pass" the halfbacks drop to cover the deep outside zones. On wide running plays to their side they must come up to the outside and turn the play inside. If a wide running play develops away from them, they revolve and become the safety man.

The safety lines up in the middle of the offensive formation and eight to ten yards deep. On the show of pass he retreats to cover the deep center zone favoring the "flow" of the developing pattern or the wide side of the field. The safety should look to the quarterback, and because of his depth, he can see the receivers on both sides by peripheral vision. On the snap of the ball he will step back and cut in the direction of flow. If there is no flow, he should continue backwards two or three steps while continuing to read. He must remember that "safety" means to play it safe. He must think in terms of pass defense first. He should *expect* long passes and be ready to play center field.

The linebackers in the wide-6 take a position directly in front of the offensive tackles at a depth of one-three yards depending upon the game situations. They generally key the tackles and on "pass" will drop back to cover the hook zones.

The defensive ends will line up about two yards outside the offensive ends and on the line of scrimmage. They look to the near back, yet must be conscious of the movements of the quarterback and the offensive end on their side. On the snap of the ball, the end takes a shuffle step across the line and if the play is coming toward him, he gains depth in the backfield, playing the outside blocker and forcing the ball carrier to the inside. On flow away from him the end backs out and rotates through the flat area to the halfback's position and finally through the safety as he moves in his pursuit route.

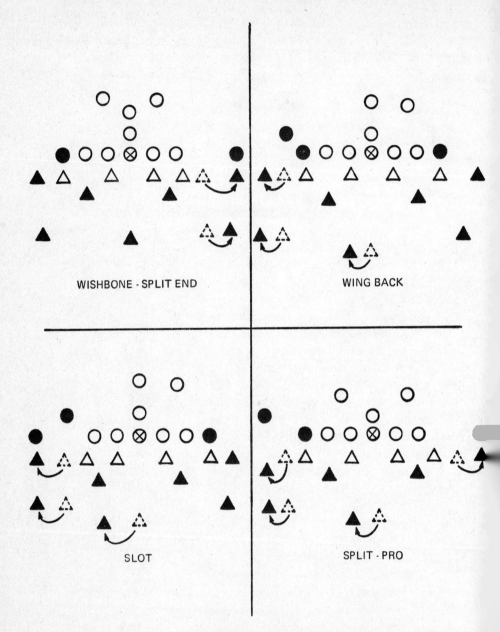

Diagram 7-4

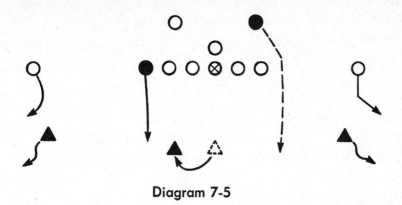

Diagram 7-5

When a drop-back pass shows, the end turns to his outside and sprints to a point eight-ten yards deep in his flat zone. He keeps his eyes on the quarterback, maintains proper horizontal and vertical relationships with receivers in his zone and plays the ball when it is thrown.

A variety of adjustments of the wide-6 to offensive sets are shown in Diagram 7-4.

The defensive end will play a split end head-on up to five yards, then he may drop off the line three-four yards and play slightly inside of him, covering the flat zone and protecting against the sweep.

On that side from which two receivers can release deep most quickly, the safety tends to shift to a position opposite the offensive guard. He will generally shift away from a split end and toward a flanker, wingback, or slotback, keying the second receiver in from that sideline. He must be careful not to overshift too far, particularly when a running back remains on the side of a split end. Receivers may come into his zone from either side (Diagram 7-5). Information from scouting reports of a particular opponent will of course refine all adjustments.

MEETING OFFENSIVE OVERSHIFTS

The simplest way to meet an offensive overshift in any defense would appear to be a rotation of the backfield (Diagram 7-6), but if this technique were to be used with the three-deep zone, it would destroy the philosophy that the responsibilities of the three deep backs should never be changed.

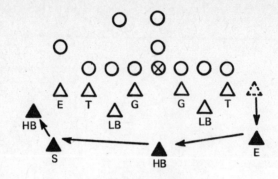

Diagram 7-6

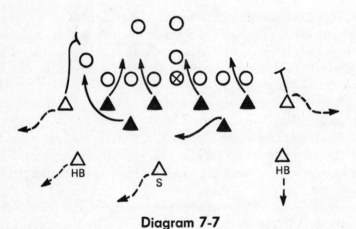

Diagram 7-7

Obviously, such an adjustment creates some new problems for the pass defense coach. Both defensive ends must now learn how to play their deep outside, the safety must also learn the techniques of both deep outside zones and each halfback must be capable of covering the flat on his side. If the personnel are capable, the problems are not too difficult, however, it may be advisable to cover such offensive overshifts with line slants and linebacker stunts (Diagram 7-7). The use of members of the forcing unit to meet overshifts is consistent with the three-deep philosophy.

You must weigh the pros and cons of various adjustment techniques in the light of the experience and abilities of the players you have available, then make your decision and stick to it. In the backfield rotation scheme the weak side flat zone is left open, while

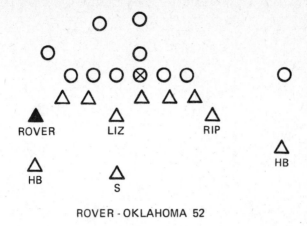

ROVER - OKLAHOMA 52

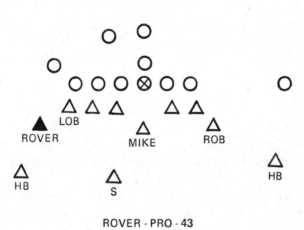

ROVER - PRO - 43

Diagram 7-8

in the use of the forcing unit one of the hook zones is usually left uncovered.

The Rover Defense

Another method of meeting overshifts without disturbing the three deep defenders is the use of the "monster" or "rover" back. The widespread use of such strong-side offenses as the wing-T, slot, strong pro, and variations of the wishbone, have made this a popular method of defense (Diagram 7-8). Its major advantage, of course, is its simplicity—most adjustments are made by

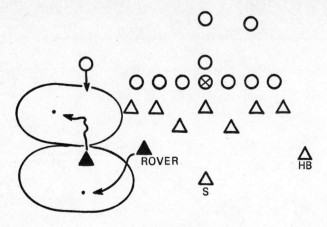

Diagram 7-9

merely relocating one man—the rover. The usual alignment priorities for rover are: (1) strong side; (2) open side; and (3) tendencies. In other words, if the offense is unbalanced, he plays on the strong side. If the offensive team is balanced in strength, he will play to the open side of the field or, if the ball is in the middle of the field, he will play where the opponent's down and distance tendencies indicate. His normal zone pass defense responsibility is the flat to his side.

Incorporating a rover defense in a three-deep zone pass defense system affords an opportunity for the development of a few secondary stunts to help disguise the coverage and confuse enemy quarterbacks. These diversions may be indicated by a defensive call and accomplished on the snap of the ball regardless of the nature of the developing play, or they may be precalled and executed only on a pass key.

Diagram 7-9 illustrates a simple stunt involving a switch of assignments between rover and the left halfback. Such an assignment for the rover implies the capacity of enough speed to cover the deep outside zone.

If one of the inside linebackers is endowed with enough speed to cover the safety position temporarily, the rover blitz shown in Diagram 7-10 can be very effective in a running situation when an off-tackle or sweep play is expected. The strong-side halfback moves up to cover the rover's flat zone if a pass develops. The safety moves over to pick up the deep outside—an assignment

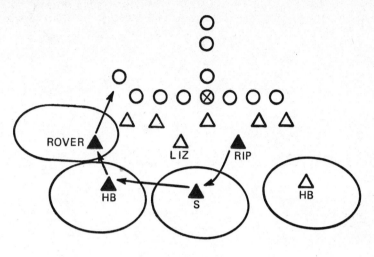

Diagram 7-10

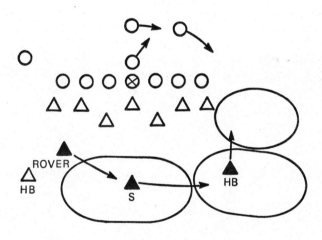

Diagram 7-11

that cannot be accomplished effectively if there is a wide split receiver to the rover side.

A stunt-rotation back to the weak side, utilizing a rover, is illustrated in Diagram 7-11. This movement can be accomplished quickly before the snap to counteract an offensive backfield shift or man in motion, or it can be done on the snap as a secondary stunt.

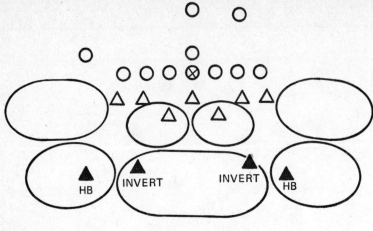

Diagram 7-12

The Invert

With the increased use of offensive backfield shifts, automatics, and the development of effective attacks to the weak side (especially option plays and sprint out passes), rover defenses have become hazardous. Too frequently, Rover is on the wrong side as the play develops. For this reason, many coaches have adopted the invert defense (Diagram 7-12). The name derives from the inversion of four deep backs. Its appeal lies not only in its flexibility but also in the fact that it retains the three-deep zone principles. Despite the fact that it presents four deep backs, the invert is fundamentally a three-deep zone. The two outside zones are covered by the halfbacks while the deep center zone is covered by one of the two safeties or invert backs. The other invert moves to cover the flat zone on his side. Some coaches have the invert on the strong side move to the flat on the show of a drop-back pass while the weak-side invert drops to cover the deep center zone. Other techniques are to have the invert backs move to the open side of the field or to offensive tendencies.

The advantages of the invert are its presentation of a "balanced look" and its ability to react appropriately to the developing play. To accomplish the latter the movement of the invert backs must be based upon an offensive key. For example, against a pro-spread both inverts may key the running back. As he moves to the strong side, the invert on that side moves up and toward the flat.

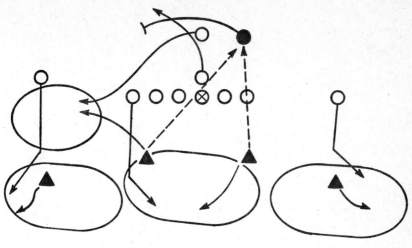

Diagram 7-13

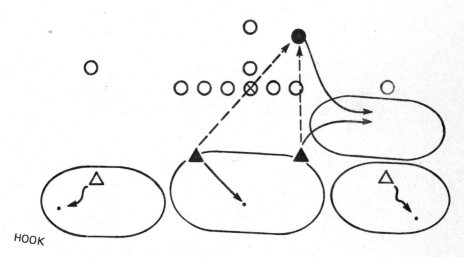

Diagram 7-14

The opposite invert moves to the deep center zone. If a sweep develops to the strong side, the strong invert continues on his route attacking the play from the inside out. If a pass develops, he levels off to protect the flat zone (Diagram 7-13). The same reactions on the snap of the ball can be made to the weak side, both inverts keying the running back (Diagram 7-14).

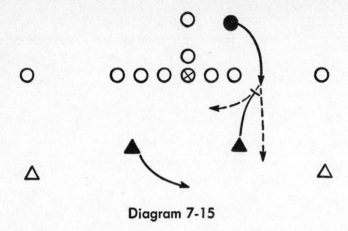

Diagram 7-15

Against a pro-spread, the invert is particularly strong on the weak side since the invert back can run a collision course with his key, the running back. By this technique he can destroy the halfback's attempts to release on the circle-middle or the circle-up patterns (Diagram 7-15). On flare and swing passes it is a simple procedure to level off in the flat, maintaining a vertical position on the halfback. If the back is the lead blocker for the fullback sweep or the quarterback rollout, the inside-out angle of the invert's collision course puts him in ideal position to play the blocker and scrape off to the ball carrier.

On drop-back passes when the running back stays in as a part of the passer protection cup, the invert backs should react to whatever tendencies are indicated by the scouting reports. It may be advisable to move to the open field, toward the weak side, to the strong side, or perhaps drop back to play a four-deep zone.

The invert lends itself to a number of stunts, but particularly the safety blitz because the invert backs are close to the line of scrimmage in the pre-snap alignment.

The simplicity and security of the three-deep zone are strong points in its favor as a pass defense system. Many coaches feel that it is the defense that offers the simplest adjustments to all flanker and spread-end situations. They are willing to sacrifice its limitations in secondary stunts and disguises to attain the proficiency that can result from simplicity. By playing the same three-deep defenders in the same positions on every down the margin of error is narrowed for the possibility of a long pass completion—and that is the kind that hurts the most.

Chapter 8

EMPLOYING THE FLEXIBLE
FOUR-DEEP ZONE

It is simple arithmetic that you can cover the field with four men better than three, and for that reason many coaches are now employing the services of four deep backs. This arrangement not only facilitates the four-deep zone, but also affords a diversity of other coverages without tipping off the opponent. From the four-deep one can play four-deep zone, three-deep zone, man-for-man, or combination man and zone coverages. Many coaches today feel that to be sound in the secondary a team must blend three-deep and four-deep principles with man-for-man and zone tactics. All quarterbacks are being taught to read deep secondary coverage now, so it becomes more important to have a variety of coverages and be able to disguise them.

The four-deep has the advantages of the three-deep Rover defense without the disadvantages. One can declare strength to the formation, tendencies, or field position before the snap, as is done in the Rover defense, or one can rotate after the snap to the point of attack, based upon offensive keys. The four-deep, like the invert, allows you to put strength where strength is needed.

Adjustments to offensive shifts and the man-in-motion can be made easily with the deep backs, not disturbing the linemen and linebackers. This factor can contribute to the simplicity of the overall defensive scheme.

It is easier to play man coverage with four deep backs in the defense than with three. The alignment itself makes it easier to adjust man coverages to the variety of offensive formations employed today, and because of its variety of faces, the four-deep is very adaptable to stunts and blitzing.

Probably the biggest single factor in the widespread adoption of the four-deep alignment is the inability of the three-deep to provide adequate change-ups against the many forms of spread offense being utilized today. With little ability to disguise itself, and the growing proficiency of quarterbacks at all levels to read and exploit defensive weaknesses, the standard three-deep alignment is rapidly fading. Notice, I did not say that the three-deep *zone* is fading, for if anything, it is gaining in stature as it becomes a vital part of most four-deep schemes.

But four-deep zone coverage has also gained an important niche in pass defense systems today. By dividing the deep area into quarters and assigning a back to each zone, this defense can maintain the advantages of deep zone coverage while retaining flexibility and the elements of surprise and disguise. This coverage is particularly good against certain offensive formations, especially those that place wide split receivers at both ends of the offensive formation (Diagram 8-1).

The slot-spread with both ends split, for example, is quite popular and could be defended by the four-deep zone as illustrated in Diagram 8-2. The position of the left outside backer permits him to play the flat zone and Y on the slant-in. He is also in good position to force-contain on run-flow to his side. The Mike man must move quickly on the snap to the strong hook zone to react to #4 on the hitch or hook patterns. As he moves, he must check the hole between his left tackle and left end in the event a run develops. The defensive left tackle, meanwhile, will loop to the center-guard gap to cover the area vacated by Mike.

The right outside backer checks #2 as he moves to the flat. If #2 swings wide, ROB will pick him up in the flat and the right corner back should then be alert to X running a coordination pattern to the inside, perhaps a break-in or a curl. If #2 swings quick up the middle ROB should look for the hitch or quick slant to X, while the weak safety picks up #2 in his zone.

The left corner and strong safety must be prepared to cover Y and #4 on deep crossing patterns, the corner covering outside and the safety covering inside. As a matter of fact, against these formations in which the four-deep zone is most effective, one might say that the pass defense secondary consists of two units. The left corner, strong safety, and left outside backer form one coordinated

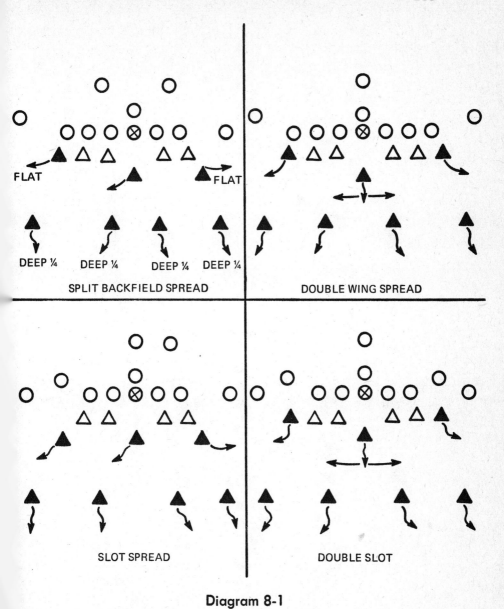

Diagram 8-1

unit, while the right corner, weak safety, and right outside backer form the other.

It may be desirable on occasion to rotate the four deep, but still maintain a four-deep alignment. Such a tactic may be utilized to gain double coverage on a dangerous receiver or to compensate for a particular offensive set or field position. The usual purpose of

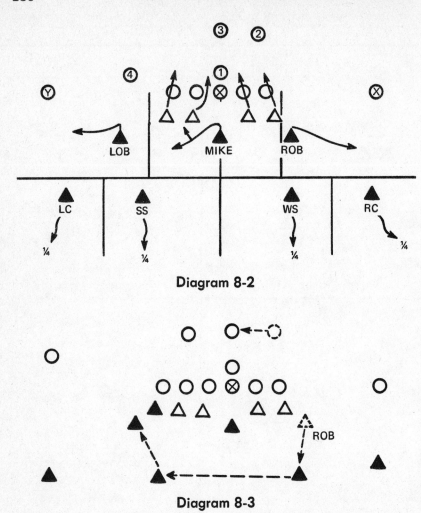

Diagram 8-2

Diagram 8-3

rotation is to get a man in a flat zone backed up by a deep outside pass protector. We most frequently associate "rotation" with the three-deep zone defense or a four-deep rotating into a three-deep. Quite often, however, the need arises to rotate strength from a four-deep alignment and still maintain four backs in the deep positions. Offensive backfield shifts that quickly move the formation strength from one side to the other may call for such a rotation. Diagram 8-3 illustrates a type of rotation from a Pro-43 which could provide a quick adjustment to a backfield shift in the pro-spread formation.

A similar rotation can be accomplished from the Oklahoma

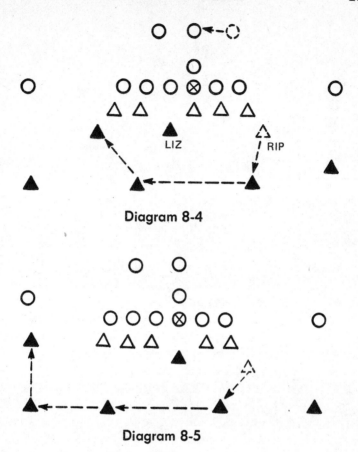

Diagram 8-4

Diagram 8-5

defense (Diagram 8-4). On the split-end side, the defense was in an Eagle adjustment with the right inside backer playing outside. In the rotation, he drops off to pick up the weak side (free) safety's zone.

If double coverage is desired on the split halfback the rotation can be accomplished as in Diagram 8-5.

As with any rotation, these movements of personnel can be made before or on the snap; however, the four-deep alignment facilitates rotation by reducing the distance that each man must move, thereby making it easier to rotate on the snap. Holding the adjustment or rotation until the ball is snapped forces the offense to read your coverage as the pattern develops. By playing a variety of coverages and adjustments you place an added burden on the offense.

A major advantage of the four-deep alignment is the speed

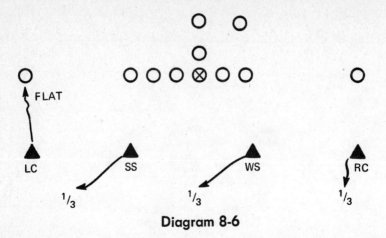

Diagram 8-6

with which it can rotate to a variety of three-deep zone coverages. The simplest method of rotation is to merely revolve the deep backs in the desired direction by bringing the corner back up to the flat, sliding the adjacent safety to cover the deep outside one-third on the side of rotation and then bringing the other safety and corner back over to pick up the deep center and opposite deep outside zones respectively (Diagram 8-6).

The difficulty in four-deep rotation lies in having the personnel to play the corner backer positions. They must be agile and fast enough to cover deep outside, yet strong and rugged enough to play the flat and attack outside running threats. Most defensive secondary coaches in selecting their personnel will determine their corner backs first. They must be the best men you have because a good offensive team will test them first.

A technique of rotation from four-deep that I have found quite successful is illustrated in Diagram 8-7. Rather than merely moving up to the flat and passively waiting for something to happen, I like to move the corner back up and into the split halfback with the intention of attacking his pass pattern. It is a pressing zone technique and in this coverage the left corner back and the left outside backer will both use it. The result is a delay of the receivers and a denial of certain routes which will assist other defenders in their coverage.

The left corner back rotates up on the snap, maintaining an outside leverage on the split halfback. He meets the receiver with his inside foot forward, keeping his alignment on the outside hip of the receiver. If the receiver breaks in or out, the defender must shuffle and slide to keep the relative outside hip position. He must

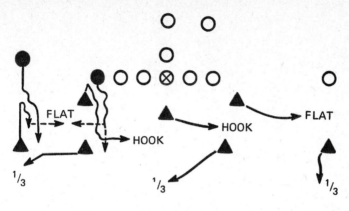

Diagram 8-7

get in the receiver's path so that he must run over or around the defender. The corner back does not step into the split back with the intention of knocking him down, but rather he wants to cushion the impact. He should carry his arms in front of him with the hands chest high, fingers up, and when contact is finally made, he should push off from the receiver, bouncing back into a balanced position still denying the receiver an outside cut, thus allowing the rotating strong safety to easily pick him up as he continues deep. At this point, the corner back must look to the tight end. If he is not moving to the flat zone, then the defender can fall off with the split halfback, harassing him on any outside cut. If the tight end threatens the flat zone, the corner back releases to pick him up.

The left outside backer helps the corner back by delaying the tight end and denying him a quick release to the flat if that is his intention. On the other hand, if the end is attempting to release downfield, the backer uses the same pressing technique employed by the corner back, denying him an outside cut as he drops off to his hook zone.

The strong safety need not drop-step and retreat to his usual zone point in rotating over to the deep outside. Because of the delayed receivers he can work laterally to his zone and pick them up at the front edge of the deep outside if they continue downfield.

A good change-up to the four-spoke rotation is the action illustrated in Diagram 8-8. This is essentially the same technique employed by the invert defense. The onside safety picks up the flat zone, the offside safety rotates to deep center responsibility.

If the split end is an outstanding receiver, rotation such as indicated in Diagram 8-9 can provide a double coverage in the

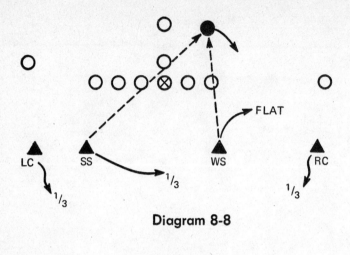

Diagram 8-8

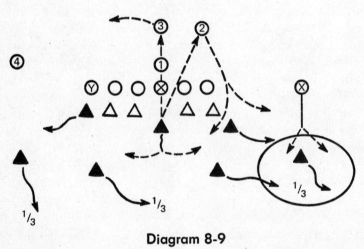

Diagram 8-9

deep outside zone. The right corner and weak-side safety can bracket X as he maneuvers in the deep outside zone while the strong safety and corner back rotate to cover the other two deep zones.

The right outside backer moves to the flat as he keys the onside halfback. The Mike man retreats on a drop pass reading the two remaining backs. If #2 releases on a circle pattern, he slides to the right to pick up that hook zone: if #3 releases to his side, Mike moves to the left hook zone looking for the tight end on the quick pass or a hook.

An effective rotation to the strength of a slot formation is

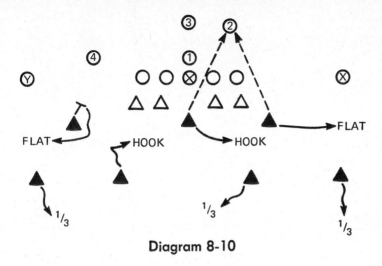

Diagram 8-10

shown in Diagram 8-10. The left outside backer takes a position to maintain outside leverage on the slot man and deny the hitch and slant passes to "Y." MIKE and ROB key #2 as they move to the hook and flat zones respectively. ROB covers the quick passes to X and picks up #2 if he swings to that side. MIKE covers #2 if he runs the circle hook pattern and will look for "X" on an inside cut if #2 swings outside.

The strong side safety shuffles forward while maintaining an inside leverage on the slot back. If #4 slants or swings to the outside, he anticipates an inside break-in or a curl pattern by "Y." The left corner, weak safety, and right corner drop to pick up the three deep zones.

The safety blitz is an effective surprise weapon that can be run best from 4-deep alignment. Any one of the four deep backs can be used as the shooter and a wide variety of patterns can be developed, depending upon the type of offensive sets and pass systems being attacked.

Diagram 8-11 illustrates a weak-side safety blitz versus a pro-spread. The weak safety should "cheat up" in his alignment, but not enough to indicate his intentions. His concentration should be on the ball so that he can explode into the blitz the moment the center snaps it. As he makes penetration he should avoid blockers rather than attempting to overpower them. His agility and the surprise of the blitz are his best weapons. He should slide between blockers and roll off blocks on his way to the passer. He should

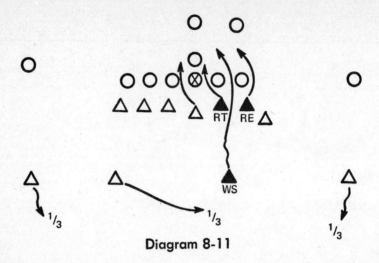

Diagram 8-11

utilize his speed, quickness, and head and shoulder fakes, taking the most direct route to the ball.

The safety blitz, like most other defensive maneuvers, must be well coordinated. As indicated in Diagram 8-11, the right tackle and right end are looping to draw the offensive guard and tackle away from the weak safety's path. A similar coordination is shown in the strong safety blitz illustrated in Diagram 8-12. Here we see the left end and tackle shifted inside to a 43 offset alignment. The left end's position assures that he will draw the block of the offensive tackle thereby opening a lane on his outside for the strong safety blitz.

An analysis of scouting reports and opponent's films must be made to determine the most effective type of blitz to use against a given opponent. One must determine their pass tendencies to establish when to blitz, then study their passer protection to determine how to blitz. Where and when are they most vulnerable for this tactic?

At best, the blitz is a calculated risk since strong pass coverage has been sacrificed to gain an additional rusher on the quarterback. Adjustments must be made in the coverage plan to compensate for the loss of a defender. In Diagram 8-11, for example, the right outside backer may have to be assigned to #2 on a man-for-man basis if he releases since there is no one left to cover the hook zone on that side. If #2 stays in as a blocker, the ROB can move to his usual flat zone assignment.

The safeties in a four-deep can also be used to support

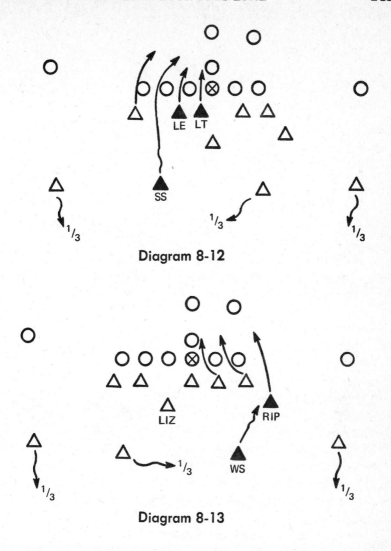

Diagram 8-12

Diagram 8-13

line-backer stunts whether employed against a run or a pass. By using a safety to pick up the stunting linebacker's original responsibility, a little insurance is gained. Stunting, like blitzing, is a gamble and the cover-up safety can reduce the odds. Diagram 8-13 illustrates a weak safety employed as support to a linebacker stunt from an Oklahoma defense. The weak safety would move on the snap of the ball to a position from which he could assume the RIP man's responsibilities for the running game. If a pass develops, his coverage would be whatever had been determined for RIP.

In Diagram 8-14, the weak safety is supporting a Mike stunt

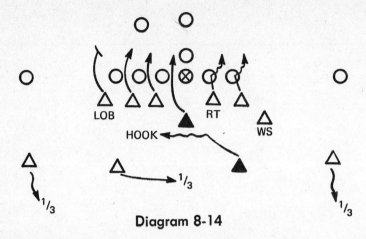

Diagram 8-14

against a strong set formation tendency that indicates "run." As he moves into position he would check the hole left open between Mike and his right tackle. If no play shows in this area, he will level off and play Mike responsibilities. If a drop back pass were to develop, he would drop to cover the strong-side hook zone while the other three backs would cover the three deep zones. Since the left outside backer is taking outside run responsibility in the stunt, the strong-side safety, who would be keying the tight end, would move up inside as flow came to their side. As one can see, the four-deep alignment affords unlimited possibilities to enhance the strength of the running defense as well as the pass defense.

Probably the greatest variety of pass coverages from the four-deep alignment can be developed from combining zone and man-for-man assignments. The four-deep zone can be combined with man-for-man or combination coverages by the linebackers, or one of the four-deep defenders can play a man assignment while the other three play three-deep zone.

Diagram 8-15 illustrates a four-deep zone and combination linebacker coverage against the pro-slot with split backs.

In this defense, Mike would key the strong-side halfback and cover him man-for-man if he released on a circle route to his side. The ROB would key and cover the left halfback all the way. The four deep backs are protecting the four deep zones. In effect, the weak-side safety will most likely be involved in double coverage since he will be picking up #2 if he releases deep, or providing the inside coverage on "X" if #2 breaks out. The left outside backer checks run-flow to his side as he checks the slot man from the outside, then moves to flat zone responsibility.

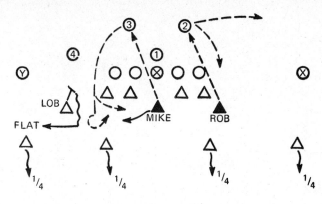

Diagram 8-15

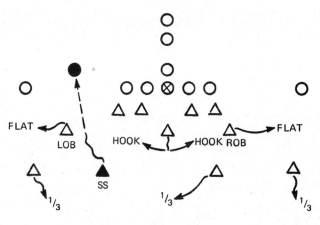

Diagram 8-16

It may be advantageous on occasion to assign one of the four deep backs to a man-for-man coverage. You may wish to cover an outstanding receiver with an outstanding defender, leaving the other three deep backs covering zone. This tactic can assure against mismatches that may result from playing a straight deep zone, and will provide automatic double coverage on the man-for-man receiver regardless of which deep zone he may enter (Diagram 8-16).

Another combination coverage that has developed from the four-deep alignment is the two-deep zone illustrated in Diagram 8-17. It can provide a very tough man-for-man defense on all five receivers yet it is protected deep by the two safeties in zone coverage.

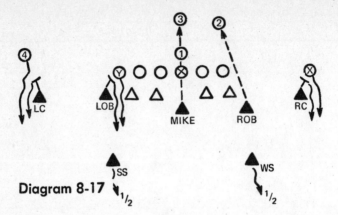

Diagram 8-17

The corner backers must crowd the split receivers a yard off the line of scrimmage, forcing them to the outside while covering them in a tight man-for-man. They must be especially aggressive in contacting these men, maintaining an inside position on them and not allowing a cut back to the inside.

The tight end must also be played with bump-and-run technique by the outside backer, while the two safeties cover the deep zones, each being responsible for one-half of the field.

This defense is especially effective in the third down situation when there is less than ten yards to go and the offensive quarterback likes to throw short passes, sidelines, slants, hooks, and hitches.

The four-deep alignment provides a great deal of versatility and a sound base from which a great many adjustments can be made to the variety of offensive sets in use today. Naturally, one would not attempt to incorporate all of the defensive variations that I have outlined in this chapter into a single defensive scheme. One defends a *specific* offense and a *specific* team, so it behooves the defensive coach to thoroughly analyze his opponent's offense and personnel and select those variations of his basic defense which will make the greatest contribution to stopping that particular team. If one or two secondary stunts are added for a given game, they should have a definite purpose, and the defensive signal caller should understand the circumstances under which he will employ them. The same must be said for new methods of rotation and adjustment that are added. Simplicity is the key to all coaching, and as much as possible, pass defense must be made simple in alignment, assignment, and execution, yet appear to the opponent as complex and confusing.

Chapter 9

THE FOUR-DEEP MAN-FOR-MAN—
INDIVIDUAL PLAY

A decade ago I wrote an article entitled, "Basic Considerations in Installing the Pro-Spread T," for one of the leading magazines of the coaching profession. The gist of this article, written during the fall of the split-T and the rise of the wing-T, was to focus attention on the pro-spread as an offense that could be operated successfully by high school and college teams. Many people today would agree with me that the most significant trend in offensive football in the past decade at these levels has been the widespread adoption of the pro-spread type offenses. Several college teams in recent years could have held their own among the professionals of ten years ago, and many high school quarterbacks today, trained in pro offensive philosophy and techniques, are superior to their college counterparts of yesteryear.

Following upon these successful advances in offense, the next significant development in high school and college football has been the widespread adoption of the pro-type, four-deep pass defense as an integral part of their defensive systems.

Many of the colleges have already adopted the pro-type defenses, but many still cling to the eight-man fronts with a three-deep secondary. The type of offense dominant in one's conference or league strongly influences the type of defense that will be employed. Where heavy emphasis on the running game exists, the eight-man front defenses will survive, but as the offenses continue to become more balanced or pass-oriented, a switch to the four-deep alignments will be made.

I doubt that many football teams at any level are playing a pure four-deep man-for-man pass defense. To do so would be to ignore one of the major advantages of being in the four-deep alignment—flexibility. The man-for-man coverages from this alignment should be only a part of the defensive package which for full effectiveness would include zone and combination coverages, thereby providing the disguise and deception necessary to attack today's sophisticated pass offenses.

THE BASIC FOUR-DEEP MAN-FOR-MAN

To get on common ground let us look at the basic four-deep man-for-man secondary as it is used with a pro-43 defense (Diagram 9-1) against a balanced pro-spread offensive alignment.

The tackles and ends, of course, are the constant forcers of the defense and may be joined from time to time by one or more of the linebackers or deep secondary when executing stunts or blitzes.

In a pure man-for-man, the middle linebacker, "Mike," would be assigned to the fullback. The strong-side outside backer may also be assigned to the fullback or could be assigned to the tight end on shallow patterns. The weak-side outside backer is assigned to the running back and will cover him on all shallow patterns such as the flare, swing, and circle-hook.

The strong-side corner back takes the split-back, and the strong-side safety covers the tight end. The weak-side corner back is assigned to the split-end while the weak-side safety, the "free" safety, picks up the running back if he comes deep.

If on a drop-back pass a defender's assigned man does not release into the pattern, but rather becomes a part of the passer protection, that defender has a secondary assignment to assist an adjacent teammate or cover a specific area or zone. The weak-side safety most frequently has this opportunity, thus the term "free" safety. Also, this man can most easily be relieved of his normal assignment to become a true free safety employed in a zone technique, used in a safety blitz, or to assist an adjacent deep defender in a double coverage. If any of these assignments are made, the weak-side backer must take full responsibility for the running back.

In Chapter 2, I cited a number of advantages and disadvantages of man-for-man pass defense. It may be well for the reader to review these at this time. I believe the most important advantage

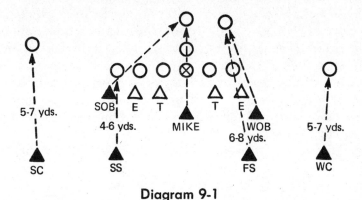

Diagram 9-1

of man-for-man is its simplicity, but its greatest disadvantage is the requirement for players with above average speed. Not only does one need players in the starting defensive backfield with speed, but it is also essential to have at least one or two capable reserves who can enter the game without hurting the team.

The Necessary Ingredient—Speed

Speed is the factor that limits the use of the pure four-deep man-for-man. The professionals, of course, have the advantage in this department. If their club needs more speed, they can always buy it, but the high school or college coach must work with what he has. I feel, however, that most teams have *adequate* speed to warrant the use of a pure man-for-man as a change-up, and certainly they have one or two boys fast enough to develop several good combination coverages to augment a basic zone coverage.

But I do not want to minimize the requirement for speed in man-for-man coverage. Not many years ago, the maximum depth of a pass depended upon the speed of the receivers, but today it relates to the strength of the quarterback's arm. Many teams, including high school teams, have receivers who can run faster than the average passer can throw in the five or six seconds that may elapse between the snap of the ball and the time the ball hits the receiver's hands. Without speed, the defensive back will find it difficult to keep up with these receivers, but with speed he can be a bothersome, pressing type player who can occasionally make a mistake and still recover to thwart a pass attempt. Harassment by fast and quick defenders enables the defense to pressure the offense into committing mistakes which can result in interceptions.

Another problem of man-for-man defense is the isolation of a defender that may occur in certain types of pass patterns. In zone defense, help is generally not far away, but in the "man" defense a back may occasionally find himself 20 to 25 yards from his nearest teammate. If this defender is too slow to cover his assigned man and lets the receiver get behind him, it's "Katie, bar the door," for a sure six points will depend only upon the passer's ability to deliver the ball.

But whatever speed is present among the football players of a given squad, I am confident it can be improved upon. The coach must make his players speed conscious and encourage them to improve through practice. Running form should be emphasized to eliminate all excessive body actions such as elbow flapping and cross-arm movement, and to correct such errors as low arm carriage and too long or too short strides.

Short sprints and relay races must be worked into the daily football practice schedule, but improvement upon natural speed can be accomplished best in the "off" season. There is no secret about it nor is there any easy way to achieve it—increased speed will result from daily running, constantly striving to eliminate excess body movements, developing better coordination, and increasing the stamina. Weight training that will develop the strength and power of the legs should be a part of the program as well as light weights used with rapid, maximum repetitions to improve reaction time.

Twenty-and 40-yard wind sprints should be run every day. Twenty to 30 of these short bursts should be run daily after the backfield candidate has conditioned his legs for it. He must think "speed" as he gets set for each of these starts, and he must explode out of his stance.

During the spring months a chart can be kept on all football candidates reflecting their weekly times in the 20- and 40-yard sprints. Develop competition among your players. Post a ladder indicating the speeds recorded for the candidates at each position of your varsity next fall.

The ability to sprint backwards is important in man-for-man defense—as important as it is to your zone defense. Some work in running backwards, should be done every day during the season since the defensive back usually starts his coverage in this manner. Drill in the skill can be included easily in the pre-practice warm-up or post-practice wind sprints. Get a stop watch time on all backfield candidates to check improvement and stimulate competition. I have found 1.4 seconds to be good time for ten yards and 2.3 seconds good for 15 yards.

Quick reactions of the hands and feet are real assets for the man-for-man defender. Like a good basketball player, he should guard the opponent "with his feet," maintaining proper position and maneuvering with the receiver as he runs his pattern. Quick hands are important in making quick changes of direction, shoving the receiver off his stride, making interceptions, fending off blockers, and scooping up loose balls. Two of the best off-season activities to develop these skills are basketball and handball. One- or two-man basketball played on half-court is better than the regular game since it requires constant one-on-one coverage.

PERSONNEL REQUIREMENTS OF THE FOUR DEEP BACKS

The foundation of man-for-man pass defense rests upon the four deep backs. How much flexibility can be developed from the four-deep alignment depends upon the qualifications of these defenders. Each position requires a slightly different type of athlete.

The two corner backs should be the best pass defenders in a one-on-one situation since they are most frequently isolated and cover the best receivers on the offensive team, the split receivers. They must be the fastest and quickest of the deep backs and ideally should have size, height, strength, and durability to facilitate their rotation to the flat area on occasions where they can be given outside running responsibility in addition to their pass defense assignment.

The combination of these attributes in the body of one player is unique and the lack of boys to capably fill these positions generally restricts the rotation and adjustment patterns and secondary stunts that can be accomplished from the four-deep.

Many coaches like to think of their four-deep as a two-headed monster. They feel that one of the big advantages of this alignment over the three-deep with a "monster" man or Rover is that it can be rotated on a key at the snap, thereby always having the "monster" on the appropriate side without shifting a man from side to side. The problem, of course, is to obtain two corner backs with the toughness of a typical "monster" yet, with the speed and agility to cover split halfbacks and ends in a man-for-man situation.

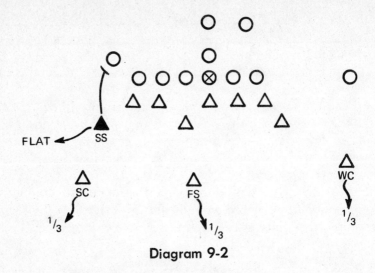

Diagram 9-2

The strong-side safety should be the best tackler of the four-deep. He is a prime support man against the run. He is frequently used in an invert technique with inside-out force responsibility on running plays to the strong side, and if the corner backs are not adequate in covering the outside running responsibility from rotation, one should be able to assign the strong safety as a "monster" man in a pre-determined three-deep adjustment when desired (Diagram 9-2).

The free safety is the quarterback of the four-deep secondary. He should be the smart, hustling, leader type ball player who can quickly recognize offensive pass patterns and direct traffic in the defensive backfield. Of the two safeties, he should be the quicker and the faster, yet he too must be a good tackler capable of moving up with authority on sweeps and power plays to the weak side.

The weak-side corner back can be the less capable of the two corners since he will frequently have assistance from the free safety and the weak-side linebacker. If the running back blocks for passer protection, the weak-side linebacker can drop off to cover the split end on shallow patterns and the free safety can assist in deep coverage (Diagram 9-3).

But this assistance cannot be depended upon, so the requirement for speed exists here as at the strong side. When the free safety and weak-side backer are tied up with their own assignments, the weak-side corner back will find himself covering the split end all by himself. He must excel in one-on-one coverage, but

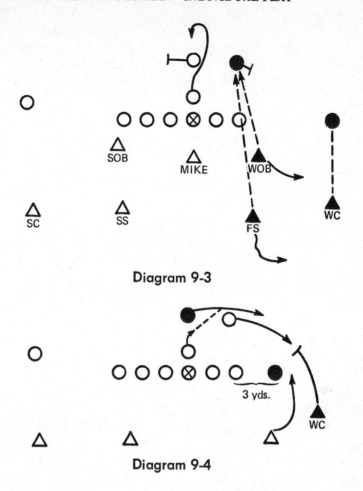

Diagram 9-3

Diagram 9-4

does not have the problem of recognizing and covering companion patterns to the same extent that the strong-side corner does.

He must be a good tackler, but since offenses run most frequently into their strong side, he will not get the amount of traffic that the strong side corner will. He must be adept at playing the split end and the running back as blockers and capable of force-contain responsibility when the split end takes a position three yards or less from his tackle (Diagram 9-4).

LINEBACKER REQUIREMENTS

The four-deep man-for-man may be played from a number of team defensive alignments, however, it is most commonly employed with the pro-43 or the Oklahoma 52. Whatever alignment is used, it should have a linebacker or defensive end at each flank who is capable of covering the near backs man-for-man on the short patterns, and the flat zone when required by the defensive scheme.

In a pro-43 defense, the strong-side linebacker normally takes a position head-up or "eye outside" the tight end. Since tight ends are selected for their size and blocking ability as well as their receiving skill, the strong-side backer must likewise have good size. At the line of scrimmage he must play like a defensive end, jamming the tight end to the inside and covering the off-tackle hole. He must never let the end hook him from the outside since he has inside-out responsibility on sweeps. These running game responsibilities imply not only good size, but also strength, quickness, and agility. Height is important since he must be able to key through the tight end and into the offensive backfield to read the near back, the quarterback, or backfield flow.

On drop-back pass plays he will play the end tough for two or three yards, delaying his release and denying him a clean break to the flat. His man-for-man assignment will be the end in the flat or the near back on flare or circle routes. How effective he will be in carrying out his pass defense responsibilities depends largely upon his speed and quickness.

The middle linebacker, as with all linebackers, has a primary responsibility to the running defense and since his combat zone is from tackle to tackle he must be an exceptional football player. He must be selected on the basis of his ability to back up the line rather than his contributions to the pass defense. His primary man-for-man assignments are the tight end, if he hooks or attempts a quick inside pass, and the fullback, if he circles tight over the tight end. Rarely will he be faced with the problem of single coverage beyond the short routes over the middle.

The weak-side linebacker can be the smallest of the three, yet he must have the greatest speed and agility. He must be capable of covering the running back one-on-one not only on circle patterns and in the flat, but also wherever he goes since the defensive scheme will frequently require the free safety to be assigned elsewhere.

When the end is split more than three yards, the weak-side linebacker becomes the force man on sweeps to his side, consequently he must be able to ward off blockers and fight his way to the ball carrier. Since he is normally backed up by the free safety in pass defense, he can be utilized in stunts more than the strong-side linebacker, providing another application of his speed and agility.

COVERAGE TECHNIQUES OF THE DEEP BACKS

Whether you use man-for-man defense or zone defense, it is mandatory for all deep backs to be able to cover one man tightly. Having become proficient in man coverage, the defenders can readily adapt to zone coverage rather than vice-versa. Naturally, many of the coverage techniques are different, but in the latter phases of a zone coverage when the deep back must commit himself to the deep man in his zone, the moves, the relationships, and the reactions can be identical. Many coaches start training their defensive backs in man coverage at the beginning of the season even though their defense may be 80 percent zone. Not only is the training in tight coverage valuable to zone defenders, but it also builds their confidence as well, to give the coach a good picture of who his best pass protectors are.

Stance is basic to all good defense. The man-for-man defender should have his feet comfortably spread with a heel to toe stagger. The knees should be flexed with a slight drop of the hips to attain a lower center of gravity. If one is playing a retreating type coverage rather than pressing, the majority of weight should be carried over the rear foot to facilitate a rapid movement backwards. Since the defender's first responsibility is pass coverage rather than the running game, he is most concerned about a quick start backwards.

Initial position should be as close to the receiver as the defender's capabilities will allow in order to discourage the quick pop passes, the hitch and slant-in. Playing tight on a fast receiver is dangerous business unless the defender can start backward quickly and accelerate rapidly in covering the streak, post, and flag patterns. To move quickly, the body weight must be carried on the back foot while the initial drive comes from the forward foot. If the weight is on the forward foot, this weight must be shifted *after* the ball has been snapped—a waste of precious time if the receiver is releasing on a deep pattern. Reaction to the running game will be a little slower with the weight back, however, split seconds in meeting this responsibility are of much less importance to the deep back than his reaction to the pass receiver.

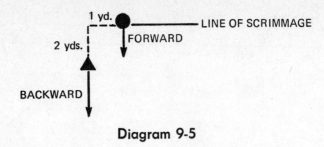

Diagram 9-5

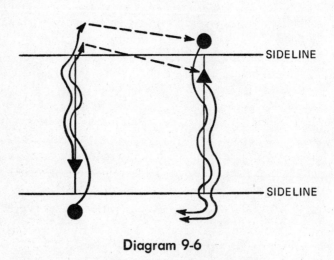

Diagram 9-6

DRILLS FOR THE MAN-FOR-MAN

After some instruction and practice in running backwards, add the drill illustrated in Diagram 9-5. Taking a position two yards ahead of the receiver, the defender should be able to stay with him for a distance of at least ten yards. Mark the point at which the receiver comes abreast and have the defender work for improvement.

The "mirror" drill in Diagram 9-6 acquaints the defender with the fundamentals of watching the receiver's moves. Have the defender take a position facing the receiver at a distance of three-four yards. On a signal the receiver releases down the 5 yard stripe, breaking left and right while the defender retreats, turning to run with the receiver, rotating his hips to match each change of direction of the receiver. He should focus his attention on the receiver's belt buckle rather than on his eyes, head, or shoulders. Since the center of gravity of the human body is between the points of the

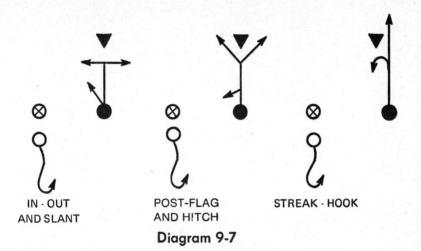

IN - OUT   POST-FLAG   STREAK - HOOK
AND SLANT   AND HITCH

Diagram 9-7

pelvis, the runner will go where his center of gravity goes, not necessarily in the direction he looks or throws his head or arms.

The next progression drill (Diagram 9-7) provides experience for the deep back in defending against specific pass routes. Have the defenders rotate from group to group so they will be exposed to each of the common routes. Add as many routes to the drill as personnel will allow.

In this drill, with the defensive backs covering from head-on position, both inside and outside cuts are possible. Under these conditions, the defender's initial steps should be directly backward. The hips drop slightly and three or four short accelerating steps are taken while still concentrating on the receiver for an early indication of his intentions. If the hitch, hook, or slant have not been indicated by this time, then the back must cross over, turn and run with the receiver, keeping two or three yards in front of him, ready to react to the final cut of his pattern. On this final leg the defensive back must move in close to the receiver, matching him stride for stride while reading the expression on his face or watching the eyes for the first indication that the ball is being thrown. At that instant, the defender himself must turn, find the ball, and adjust his position for the interception.

If interception is not possible, the defensive back must extend himself to bat the ball down. When possible this should be accomplished by reaching in front of the receiver with the offside arm. In other words, if the receiver broke to the defender's right, the defender would reach across with his left arm to bat the ball. This technique turns the defender's body into the receiver giving

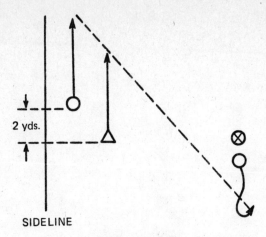

2 yds.

SIDELINE

Diagram 9-8

him good position to follow through with a tackle if the pass is completed. If he reaches in front with his onside arm and misses the ball, he will have his side or his back toward the receiver, leaving him in poor position to recover and tackle or pursue.

A drill that teaches the defensive back when to look for the ball is illustrated in Diagram 9-8. The receiver is given a two-yard start on the defender and he runs a deep streak pattern down the sideline. As he crosses the pre-determined point (15-20-25-30 yards), the quarterback throws and the receiver looks back for the ball. The defender should do likewise, looking over his inside shoulder while continuing to maintain his relative position on the receiver as he adjusts to intercept.

Surprisingly, the most dangerous receivers are not necessarily the fastest receivers. The good actor with above average speed can be a real thorn to the pass defense.

Let us look at some of the points that are generally emphasized to potential receivers:

1. Run at different rates of speed in order to confuse the defender.
2. Never run a straight line pattern.
3. Make the fake routes and the actual routes appear the same.
4. Use a variety of fakes.

In addition, against a man-for-man defense receivers are

taught to release by an angle in or out, weave, or use a change of pace to gain a favorable position on the defender. They want to move the defender, to make him commit himself so they can break away from him.

Good receivers have the ability to run at three-quarters and seven-eighths speed, yet appear to be going at full speed. They always keep a little reserve to use when they break on their final cut to move away from the defender at the crucial point.

On any deep or middle pattern, they will make at least one fake before they cut on their true pattern. Much of their practice time is spent in perfecting these fakes to make them look like the real thing. Most fakes come in the first 10-12 yards of a receiver's route because the quarterback has no more than three or four seconds to get his pass away.

The good receiver will have a complete assortment of body fakes, leg fakes, eye fakes, hand fakes, hip fakes, and fakes of the shoulders and arms. One reason that many good college broken-field runners have tremendous success in professional football as split ends and split halfbacks is because they have developed the techniques of faking and the change of pace through years of ball-carrying duties. A rookie defensive back being introduced to the mechanics of man-for-man pass defense for the first time has his hands full covering a receiver with experience in these fine arts.

Some receivers have all the tricks mastered and they show them on every play whether they are the primary receiver or not. These are the most difficult receivers to cover. Their intention is to keep the defense off balance and confused.

The defensive back in man-for-man coverage should attempt to take some of this initiative away from the receiver. By playing an offensive defense he can neutralize much of the advantage that the receiver initially holds. He must be the aggressor, attempting to make the receiver do what he, the defender, wants him to do. He should press the receiver. The ideal man-for-man defender should be capable of playing his man so tightly that he will deny him his intended pass routes or at least destroy the timing of his patterns. Hours and hours must be spent on one-on-one coverage to perfect this ability. Use your best pass receivers, those that run the best patterns, to drill against your own defensive backs. This is a type of skill development that can be accomplished in the off-season. Even in mid-winter a lot of work can be done on the gymnasium floor in developing man-for-man coverage skills.

Determining Proper Position on the Receiver

Taking the proper field position on a receiver can provide a big assist in his coverage also. The exact position the back assumes relates to a variety of factors including the game situation, team field position, offensive and defensive alignments, and down and distance. But the most important factor is the offensive man himself. This type of pass defense is reduced to a personal contest between the defender and the receiver, each trying to outsmart, out-maneuver, and outrun the other. Other things being equal, the one who has prepared himself best will win. In this respect, the defender has the advantage—he knows (or *should* know) whom he is going to defend against several days before the game. Unless the defensive alignments are minimal, unimaginative, and static from game to game, the offensive receiver will not know his personal opponent until game time and even then his defender may vary during the game.

Scouting reports should indicate the best patterns of each offensive receiver and which patterns each likes to run under different game situations. Does the split halfback like the hook or the sideline on third and long yardage? Does he have the speed for the hook and go or the streak? Which does he run the most, inside cuts or outside cuts? What are his most dangerous patterns? All of these questions and many more should be answered by the scouting reports. Additional information should be available on the opposing quarterback. What are his best throws? Does he fake well? How does he fake? How quickly does he deliver the ball?

All available films should be reviewed in detail to study the techniques the receiver uses in running his various patterns. Films and a projector should be made available to the players so they may do this in their free time—before classes, the noon hour, before or after practice. If the defensive back has a co-operative teammate, it would be good to study films together so the teammate could simulate the opponent in pre-practice or after-practice sessions.

Having studied the opponent, the defensive back can now take his field position with more intelligence than the usual guidelines provide. It is a mistake to have all backs play the same defensive position from the same point on the field; however as a general rule, the farther the split receiver is from his quarterback, the deeper the defensive back may play.

Relative speed and reactions of the two opponents will be

most important in determining the *depth* of the defensive backs initial position. Some backs can set up only three or four yards off the line of scrimmage and still cover their receiver effectively. Most will require a minimum depth of five to seven yards against a good receiver with above average speed. Each defensive back must experiment on his own against various type receivers to determine his own capabilities. If he is too cautious and lines up too deep, he will get beat on the short patterns. If he is too tight, he runs the risk of getting beat on the deep patterns. So the defender has to play as tight as his ability will allow, and there is little room for error.

Of course, down and distance influence the defensive back's position too, and the scouting reports should indicate the offensive team's down and distance tendencies. The main points to determine are those situations in which the opponent is likely to throw deep. Under these circumstances, the back may want to loosen up an extra yard or two. Certainly in the long-yardage situations this will be true. Sometimes the offensive alignment or "set" will be a tipoff on their intentions to throw certain types of passes. Field position is an indication for many teams also and they will show tendencies to throw only certain types of passes in particular areas of the field.

The score and the time remaining in the game are important. If your team is behind late in the game, your defensive backs are going to have to move in a little tighter and play for the interception all the way. They are going to have to gamble. On the other hand, if you are ahead, they can lie back a little, be more conservative, and insure against "the bomb."

Lateral position of the defensive back is also predicated on a number of factors. The outside defenders have the sideline to aid them so there is little need ever to take a position closer than five yards from a sideline regardless of how close to it the receiver may line up. The defender should maintain an inside position on a receiver who is within five yards of the sideline, and by playing him tight he can deny him the inside cuts while maneuvering him further toward the sideline and possibly out of bounds.

In a more open area of the field, the defender should take a lateral position that will aid him best in taking away the receiver's favorite patterns. If he prefers the inside cuts, then it may be advisable to play slightly inside on him. It may be even better to take an outside position to invite him into his inside cuts, then in the initial movement glide to the inside. Not many receivers are capable of running all pass patterns with equal finesse. They generally have two or three favorite cuts and the majority of their receptions will be from these cuts. Defensively, these are the patterns to deny them, and taking the appropriate lateral position can be a valuable aid.

It may be desirable to deny outside cuts in certain circumstances; particularly if there is a possibility of having help on the inside cuts from a linebacker or a free safety. In this situation, the back should take a position with the outside foot forward and favoring the outside of the receiver. As the offensive man releases, the back will immediately drop-step with his inside foot, cross over and turn to run still maintaining that outside leverage. The defender can play his man more tightly in this coverage and if their speed is equal, they may be shoulder to shoulder. If an attempt is made to break toward the sideline, the back can easily deny the route by stepping into the receiver's path. Also, from an outside position the defender can generally pick up the quarterback by peripheral vision, so if the ball has not been released, he can take this opportunity to jostle and push the receiver off stride.

By maintaining a half-yard on his opponent, the defensive back can deny the streak pattern and also put himself in a good position to play inside cuts through the receiver. As the ball is delivered on inside patterns, he must play it tough by leaping high and reaching over the receiver's shoulder with his outside arm. His interception possibilities are slim on the inside cuts because of his body position so he should concentrate on batting the ball away.

Denying the inside cuts would, of course, be similar to the outside techniques, with the back lining up to favor the inside of the offensive man and his inside foot forward. Since this encourages outside cuts where no help can be expected, this strategy is normally employed only when the receiver is near the sideline or split to the open side of the field at a considerable distance from the ball. In the latter situation, the time element involved in throwing the ball on any flag or sideline type cut to a wide split man would make the pass a hazardous one. Most coaches and quarterbacks avoid such throws; so the defensive back can afford to take an inside position under these circumstances thereby putting himself at a considerable advantage.

The Bump and Run Technique

In recent years a lot of publicity has been given to the "bump-and-run" technique of man-for-man coverage. Several professional teams developed this techniques to a fine science and at least one, the Oakland Raiders, developed an entire pass defense system around this type of coverage and were extremely successful. But as always in this game of football, the offense soon catches up with the defense whenever something new has been introduced. It did not take offensive coaches long to realize that the bump-and-run as it was being used could not be employed against a man-in-motion so this device was employed instead of setting a wide split receiver. The other weakness of which quarterbacks soon took advantage was the difficulty corner backs encountered in covering the split receiver on sideline-and-up patterns.

The original idea of bump-and-run was that a quick and fast defender could maintain tighter coverage on a receiver by playing him tight on the line of scrimmage, bumping him as he released, then matching him stride for stride, jostling him as he ran his route, and staying close enough to "bite his ear" as he drove on the final leg of his route. The technique was radical enough to surprise a great many receivers who were not prepared for it. After all, receivers have been traditionally trained to expect the defensive back to set initially 5-6 yards off the line of scrimmage and to retreat as they release, maintaining a cushion. At worst they could expect only to be interfered with at the line of scrimmage, and coaches always taught them a few techniques to counteract this delay attempt.

It took the receivers and coaches a little time to adjust, but when they did, the single coverage bump-and-run was soon discredited as a pass defense system. Coaches realized that as a constant technique it was vulnerable to well trained receivers and quarterbacks who had become familiar with it, but as a change-up or as a double-team technique it could be a valuable adjunct to a good pass defense system.

Two methods of bump-and-run have now been developed. The first and original method as described above is to attack the receiver immediately; the second method allows the receiver to release on the first leg of his route, then the defender steps into his path forcing the receiver to run over him or change his intended route.

In the attack method, the defender may take a close position on the line of scrimmage before the snap or he can disguise his intentions by lining up 5-6 yards deep, then sneaking up close just prior to the snap. All receivers whether they use a two-point or a three-point stance will turn their heads in toward the ball after they have taken their position. At this time it is possible for the defender to sneak forward enough to assure a good solid blow as the receiver comes off the line. The two-hand shiver is the best method of contact. The blow should be driven upward to straighten the receiver up and destroy his timing while the defender bounces back ready to drive with him when he recovers.

In the second method of bump-and-run, the defender holds his position at 5-6 yards off the line of scrimmage allowing the receiver to release freely. If the receiver starts a breaking movement, the defender shuffles laterally to maintain his lateral position. It is important at this stage that he does not advance or retreat. He does not want to attack the receiver nor does he want to maintain the usual cushion. The intention is to maintain a position in front of the receiver so that he must run over the defender or attempt to run around him. During this movement the feet must not be crossed, the emphasis must be on slide and shuffle. The hands are carried in front of the body, finger tips up to cushion the impact with the receiver and to shove off in the direction of the intended route. It is important at this point that the defender does not attempt to step into the receiver with the intention of knocking him down. He must be in balance ready to bounce back from the receiver and prepared to drive with him on the next leg of his route.

If the receiver slams into the defender, he should not try to bump him back but rather cushion the impact, hand fight him, and keep him from pushing off.

Discourage the defensive back from cutting the receiver's legs with a body block. Some boys resort to this technique as an easy way out. Too frequently, the ball has been thrown while the defender is concentrating on the block and a penalty results. Even if successful, the receiver usually falls on top of the defender and can scramble to his feet first and be in the clear.

In either of the bump-and-run methods the defensive back should favor one side of the receiver or the other. Some defensive schemes will prefer forcing the receiver to the inside, others will

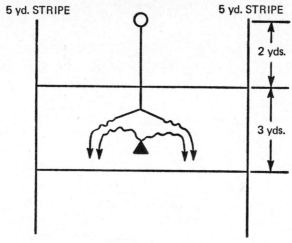

Diagram 9-9

prefer driving him to the outside. The weak-side corner back, for example, may play outside the split receiver to deny him deep outside and drive him in toward the free safety.

The drill in Diagram 9-9 provides good training and experience in the shuffle footwork, contact, and recovery utilized in the delayed style of bump-and-run. The defensive back sets up in the rear of the box, head-up on the receiver. The receiver releases straight downfield for three yards then may break left or right as he enters the rectangular box. The defender shuffles to maintain his position on the receiver, delivers a two-hand shiver at contact, recovers and drives with the receiver as he breaks downfield.

The defensive back can next be placed in an inside or an outside relationship with the receiver and trained in denying certain types of cuts inside the box. A quarterback can then be added to the drill. Have him throw after three seconds, forcing the ball to the receiver whether he is open or not, giving the defender interception experience.

It is an unusual defensive back who can be depended upon to successfully play bump-and-run in isolation, and most coaches have learned that this technique is safe only when some additional help can be provided—whether it is to the inside, the outside, or deep. The advantages of this style of play are obvious, however. Ordinarily, the defensive back is concerned with what the receiver is going to do, but an aggressive defender, mixing in a little bump-and-run technique, can get the receiver to wondering what he, the defender, is going to do next.

COVERAGE TECHNIQUES OF THE LINEBACKER

The linebackers in man-for-man defense have some special problems to be considered. Since under normal circumstances their position in the team defense is related primarily to defending the running game, the techniques they employ in pass defense will necessarily be different from those of the perimeter backs.

In his stance the linebacker usually carries the majority of his weight on the forward foot to assure strength, power, and a quick start in meeting the running threat in his area. Which foot is forward depends upon the type defense employed, position within that defense, and the coach's or player's preference. Variations in the basic stance will be necessary to meet the many defensive assignments of linebackers, but foot stagger should never be more than heel to toe. When the defense calls for a man-for-man pass responsibility in an obvious pass situation, the stance can be adjusted to provide a more equal distribution of weight. This more balanced position affords quicker lateral or backward movements which are generally the initial reactions of a linebacker to his man-for-man key.

Linebackers are generally in position to key their pass assignments through offensive linemen. As in the pro-43, the strong-side linebacker can key his onside back while still being conscious of movement of the tight end (Diagram 9-10). The Mike man keys the fullback through the center and the quarterback, and the weak-side backer can key his onside back while still watching the weak-side offensive tackle by peripheral vision.

Against specific offenses definite reactions will be assigned each linebacker, based upon the movements of his key. The primary key may be a lineman in certain situations and the assigned man for pass defense at other times.

The offensive back assigned to each linebacker for pass defense is also the back who can threaten the respective linebacker's running responsibility the quickest, consequently as he reacts to his pass key he places himself in good position to defend the run threat (Diagram 9-11).

The lateral position of the outside backers is of course determined by the team scheme of defense and in the pro-43 the outside backers are in ideal position to assume their man-for-man pass responsibilities. In other defenses, however, it may be advisa-

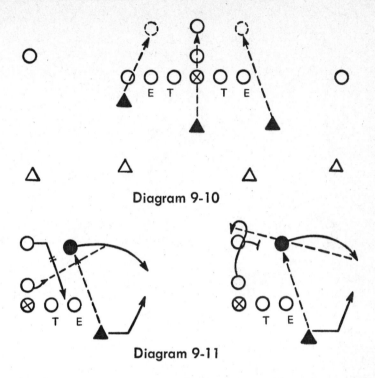

Diagram 9-10

Diagram 9-11

ble to adjust a linebacker's position to give him a more favorable alignment, particularly in obvious passing situations.

WEAK-SIDE LINEBACKER'S COVERAGE

Three favorite patterns of the weak-side linebacker's key, the running back in a pro-spread formation, are illustrated in Diagram 9-12. If this backer's lateral position is normally inside as it is in an Oklahoma 52, he is at a disadvantage in covering the swing and flare patterns. It is logical then to adjust him from time to time toward the flank where he can more readily pick up his pass responsibility, obtain better leverage, and be relieved of some interior running responsibility. From the Oklahoma defense this adjustment can be accomplished by going into an Eagle 52 spacing on the weak side, or into what some coaches refer to as a TEB (tackle-end-backer) adjustment (Diagram 9-13).

The weak-side backer can cover the halfback swing pattern best by moving laterally toward the sideline with the receiver until

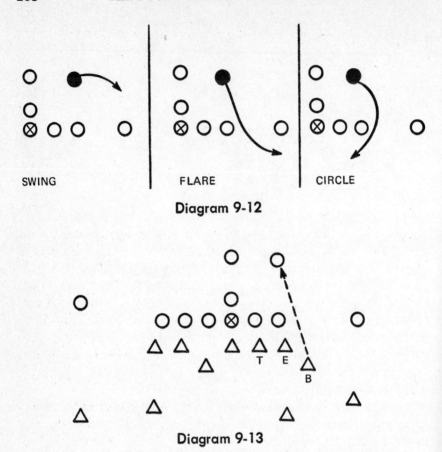

SWING   FLARE   CIRCLE

Diagram 9-12

Diagram 9-13

the ball is thrown. In single coverage it is virtually impossible for the linebacker to prevent completion of a well thrown swing pass, so the defender should think in terms of maintaining good position on the receiver to assure making the tackle almost immediately after the completion. He should *not* cross the line of scrimmage until the ball is thrown and then at an angle that will restrict the receiver from an inside cut, tackling him high with the helmet in front. Being overanxious and slanting across the line prematurely opens the door to a possible long gain from this simple behind-the-line pass (Diagram 9-14). The backer should be concerned first with maintaining good lateral position on the halfback, reacting up only when the ball has been thrown. If he moves in on the receiver too soon, the quarterback can fake the swing pass and signal the receiver on a streak pattern for a long gain.

    Probably the most difficult pattern for the linebacker to cover is the halfback *flare* into the flat. If the route is run properly

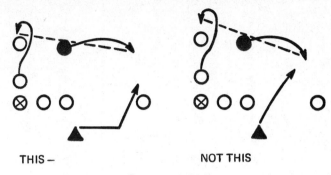

THIS—   NOT THIS

Diagram 9-14

and the pass is thrown correctly, the play is almost impossible to break up from a linebacker position. The backer should concern himself with maintaining good position to minimize the gain with a sure tackle after the completion. This may sound like a negative approach to the problem, but one must consider the offensive advantage. A flare is essentially a sideline cut run from a backfield position. Since the linebacker is inside and the final leg of the pattern is to the outside, it is impossible for the backer to move into the flight of the ball if he is maintaining sufficient depth to prevent a flare-and-up pattern.

There are several methods of running this flat pattern (Diagram 9-15 a, b, c.). From the drop-back type offense it is generally run into a split-end side where the end can be used to clear the area and the halfback can more readily get into the flat. The pattern is basic to the sprint-out or roll-out type offense in which it is run equally to both split-end and tight-end sides.

Covering the "a" and "b" techniques does not present the problems that a properly run "c" pattern can raise. In the former the receiver has committed himself early and the linebacker can do likewise, knowing that his own inside position and the angle of his route deny an inside cut. The pattern shown in "c," however, forces the linebacker into the possibility of having to cover a variety of cuts. In this route the halfback swings around the defensive tackle as close as he can without being "clotheslined." This tight swing allows him to turn straight up the field as soon as he clears the line of scrimmage, forcing the linebacker to drop back in the event a deep pattern is developing. As soon as the defender starts this backward movement, the receiver makes a quick break to the sideline. At this point the linebacker must close on the receiver by taking a sharp angle to meet him at the crossroads. As he moves in,

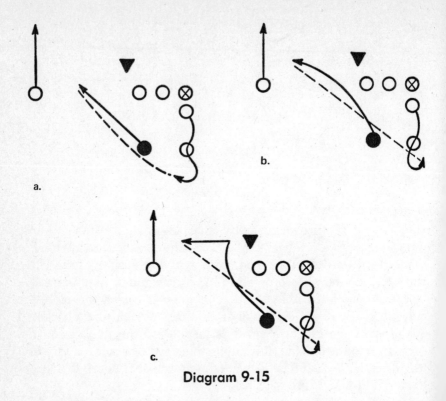

Diagram 9-15

the defender should be watching the receiver's head. If the pass is thrown properly, it will be released as the back begins his outside cut, then the ball and the defender will arrive at the reception point at the same time. A common error in covering sideline type cuts is to fall in behind the receiver, losing position and becoming a chaser (Diagram 9-16).

The weak-side backer should always maintain his inside leverage on the receiver giving him only one way to go—outside, which is the longest point from the ball. As he moves in his coverage of the swing and flare patterns, he should always be alert to helping on the slant to the split end which is frequently a companion pattern.

The simplest method of covering the halfback on a circle route is to take a collision course, attacking the receiver as soon as he clears the line of scrimmage (Diagram 9-17). Contact must be made on an inside-out angle and preferably with enough force to destroy the pattern completely by dropping the halfback. One effective method is to drive the shoulder pad high into the receiver while delivering a solid rip-up with the outside forearm into his

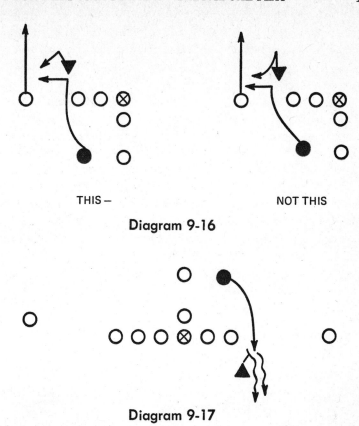

THIS—   NOT THIS

Diagram 9-16

Diagram 9-17

numbers. The linebacker must time this so he is driving forward at a slight outside angle at the moment of impact. If he lets the receiver get abreast of him, the receiver can absorb the shock by gliding to the outside. The backer should bounce back from the contact, maintain his inside leverage and be ready to drive with the receiver as soon as he recovers.

If the weak-side backer's man blocks for passer protection, he drops off to the hook zone ready to help out on short inside routes of the split-end or crossing-end patterns. He must also be alert to the screen pass and get into it quickly if it is thrown to his side.

COVERAGE BY THE STRONG AND MIDDLE LINEBACKERS

The strong-side backer in a pro-43 defense plays very much like an end in the Oklahoma 52. He must play as close to head-up on the tight end as he can without being hooked from the outside. His inside foot should be forward with the shoulders parallel to the line of scrimmage. His running responsibility is the off-tackle hole. If the end blocks down on the tackle, the backer steps up into the off-tackle hole ready to meet the play. He protects the middle linebacker by preventing the tight end from releasing unmolested on him, and he pursues sweeps to his side from the inside-out.

His man-for-man assignment is the first back out of the backfield to his side. He keys the near back through the tight end. He always plays the tight end tough. If he attempts to release downfield, the strong-side backer will fight him for 2-3 yards, maintaining outside leverage and reading the near back. He covers the swing and flare passes in the same manner as the weak-side linebacker, being alert to the slant pass to the split halfback as he moves out. His position on the tight end should deny a quick release to the flat. If he does escape, however, the backer must move out with him, maintaining his outside position and gaining depth. The near back in this situation will be picked up short by the Mike man and deep by the strong safety (Diagram 9-18).

He must be alert to the outside screen to his side, and if the near back does not release, he must get depth to the hook zone playing in front of the curl to the split halfback and watching for a crossing receiver from the weak side.

The middle linebacker, Mike, keys the fullback and picks him up if he circles over the tight end (Diagram 9-19). If he flares wide, the outside backer will cover him, but now Mike must look for the tight end on a quick pop pass (Diagram 9-20).

If the fullback stays in to block, the Mike man drops off to the strong-side hook zone gaining depth, ready to check the tight end if he attempts to cross.

The major problem of any linebacker in the man-for-man is speed. By maneuvering personnel with its formations, the offense can force a linebacker into covering a faster back. By properly calling the adjacent pass receiver routes they can compound this problem by isolating the linebacker during coverage, making support from other defenders practically nil (Diagram 9-21). Now if the linebacker gets beat, it is a sure six points.

Only two methods are available to counteract this development: (1) play the receiver loose and give up the short patterns, or (2) change the defenses frequently and disguise them so the offensive quarterback cannot anticipate the coverage and, consequently, the isolation.

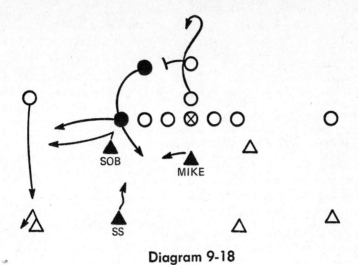

Diagram 9-18

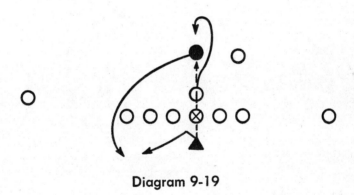

Diagram 9-19

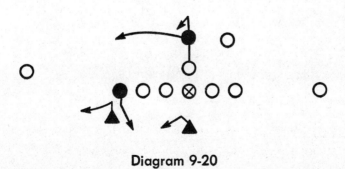

Diagram 9-20

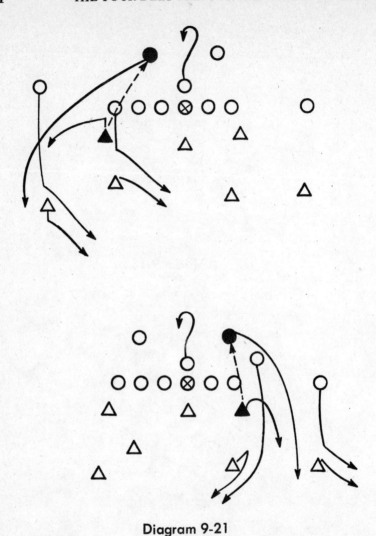

Diagram 9-21

The latter technique is desirable in most situations and a little ingenuity in defensive planning can even turn the isolation attempts into defensive advantages. By disguising a double coverage on the linebacker's key the defense can exploit the offensive quarterback's attempts at linebacker isolation.

Chapter 10

THE FOUR-DEEP MAN-FOR-MAN—
TEAM PLAY

In the development of a pass defense system that will serve a team well for the season, one must provide at least the following capabilities:

1. Provide a balanced coverage.
2. Provide double coverage on a split end.
3. Provide double coverage on a split halfback.
4. Provide an overload to the offensive strong side.
5. Provide an overload to the offensive weak side.

Obviously, no single alignment will meet all of these qualifications, so it becomes necessary to select a basic alignment from which adjustments can be made easily, quickly, and simply. The basic alignment must afford this flexibility, yet provide opportunities to disguise the defensive intentions. I believe the four-deep man-for-man most nearly meets all of these qualifications if appropriate personnel are available.

The pro-43 defense outlined in Chapter 9 utilizes the conventional four-deep balanced man-for-man pass defense. From this standard alignment a variety of adjustments can be made, limited only by the imagination and ingenuity of the coaching staff. Played in its basic form, this defense assures adequate pass coverage on every receiver and affords double coverage by those defenders whose assigned men do not release.

175

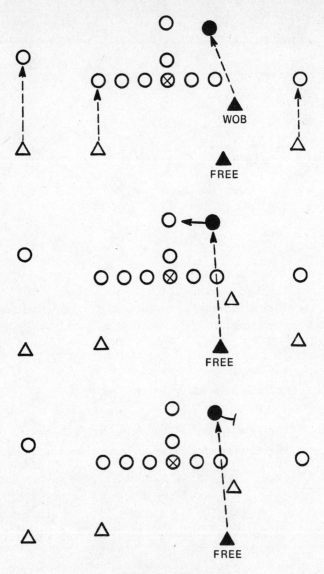

Diagram 10-1

An added advantage of the balanced four-deep is that it can provide a true free safety, an extra security feature that many coaches desire. Since the weak-side outside backer and the weak-side safety are both assigned to the running back, the safety can be released from this responsibility by a pre-determined call that transfers full responsibility to the backer. He may also be made

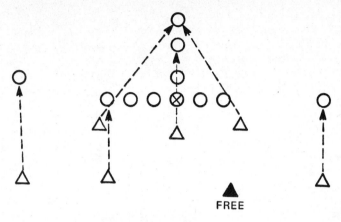

Diagram 10-2

free when the running back goes across the formation or when the running back blocks passer protection (Diagram 10-1). Against some formations the weak-side safety may be initially free because it would be unnecessary or impractical to give him a man assignment (Diagram 10-2).

BALANCED COVERAGES

The balanced four-deep can be utilized against any balanced offensive formation (Diagram 10-3). Some coaches flip-flop the corners and safeties as the offense sets left or right, keeping the same combinations always on the tight-end and split-end sides. Other coaches prefer to exchange only the safeties, feeling that the greatest difference in personnel requirements exists between the tight safety and the free safety. Against tight end-split end offenses some coaches switch the outside linebackers.

The balanced four-deep can be divided into two convenient units for training. The strong safety, strong corner, and strong outside backer constitute one unit and the weak-side safety, corner, and outside backer make up the second unit (Diagram 10-4).

The strong-side unit must be trained in covering the complementary patterns of the split halfback and the tight end. The corner back and safety must learn to work together, playing a switching man-for-man on deep crossing patterns, supporting each

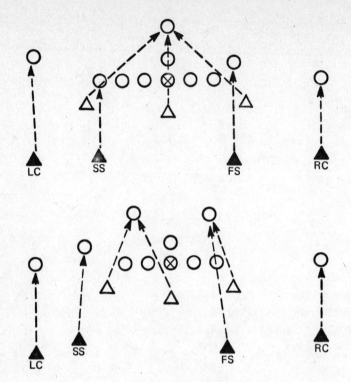

Diagram 10-3

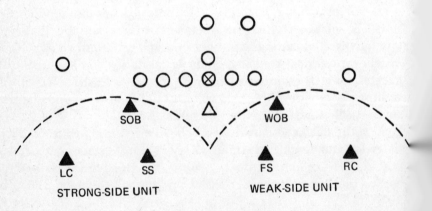

Diagram 10-4

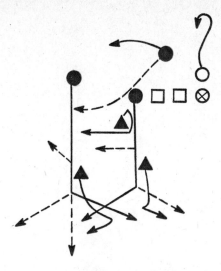

Diagram 10-5

other inside and out when a single receiver comes down, constantly talking to each other as the pass pattern develops. The strong-side outside backer makes his contribution to the unit by delaying the tight end, denying him certain cuts, covering the near back if he releases, and providing underneath coverage in the flat zone if he blocks. In the pre-season work, after the defensive backs have been schooled in the fundamental techniques of man-for-man, the next phase of training should be this unit coordination.

Acquaint your defensive backs with the common patterns that are used against these defenders and run them in the drill illustrated in Diagram 10-5. During the season substitute those patterns which scouting reports indicate are the favorites of the upcoming opponent.

The same technique should be applied to training the weak-side unit. Here the free safety and weak-side corner back need work in double covering the split end. The weak-side backer and the free safety need training in their coverage of the running back. Some complementary patterns of the running back and split end will require coordination of the weak safety and corner back in covering deep (Diagram 10-6).

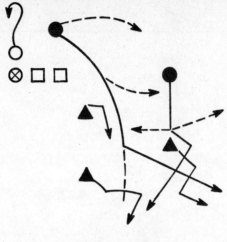

Diagram 10-6

DOUBLE COVERAGES OF THE SPLIT END

The three defenses illustrated in Diagram 10-7 provide maximum coverage on the split end by doubling him with the weak-side corner and safety. In the first defense (a), the corner back moves up on the snap to press the split end, attacking the short patterns and forcing him outside, then covering him from the inside if he drives deep. The free safety has turned full responsiblity for the running back over to the weak-side backer as he slides toward the split end maintaining inside leverage and a cushion on him, covering from the inside-out.

The second defense (b) is a change-up from the first and is particularly effective against the split end on slants, curl-ins, and hitches. The corner drops off to pick up the end deep and the free safety moves on an invert route at the snap of the ball ready to meet the end on short inside patterns. If the end releases deep, the free safety checks the running back for the flare or swing pass. The weak-side backer drops off immediately, keying the running back for the curl pattern. If this does not develop, he provides double coverage of the split end from the inside.

The third defense (c) provides a deep double coverage on the split end with the corner taking the outside cuts, the safety taking the inside. Any pass thrown to him when this coverage is on should be intercepted.

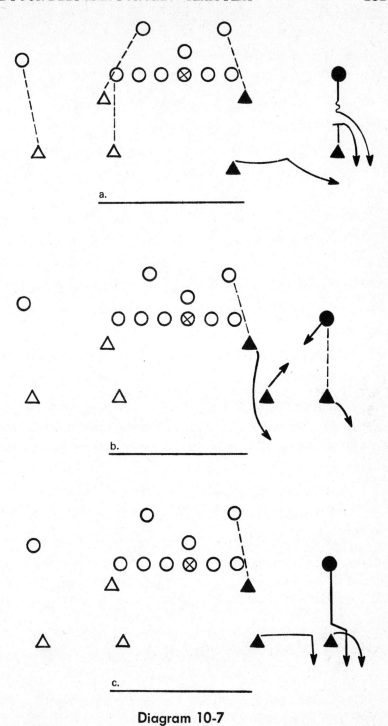

Diagram 10-7

DOUBLE COVERAGES OF THE SPLIT HALFBACK

Diagram 10-8 illustrates two methods of providing double coverage on a split halfback. In the first (a), the strong corner back moves up to press the split back, maintaining inside leverage to defend the slant or hitch passes. Prior to the snap he should cheat up to a depth of only three or four yards. If the back releases downfield, the corner will contact him with the bump-and-run technique, obstructing him, forcing him to release outside while driving with him, holding inside leverage. The strong safety provides the double coverage on the split back by maintaining a vertical cushion.

If the strong backer is capable of covering the tight end by himself, that assignment should be given to him. If help is required, the free safety can again check off the running back to the weak backer, then glide to the strong side ready to pick up the tight end if he comes deep. The strong backer must force the tight end to the inside so that he cannot release to the flat.

The second method (b) provides a double coverage, using the strong corner to provide outside cover while the strong safety provides inside cover. The strong backer and free safety play as they did in the previous method.

STRONG-SIDE OVERLOAD

As mentioned earlier, a sound pass defense must provide for an overload toward a shift of offensive formation strength. This can be accomplished by rotating the defensive backfield before the snap or by stunting into the overload on the snap. A pre-snap rotation designed to put pressure on the strong side receivers and to provide adequate coverage of strong-side flood patterns can be accomplished easily as follows:

The strong corner rotates up on the line of scrimmage taking a slight inside position on the split back. On the snap, he bumps him with a two-hand shiver and rebounds, maintaining inside leverage and watching the flow of the backfield. If a strong-side sweep develops, he is in ideal position to provide an immediate force. His pre-snap position has denied the hitch and slant-in to the halfback. He now drops off to a depth of six yards obstructing the

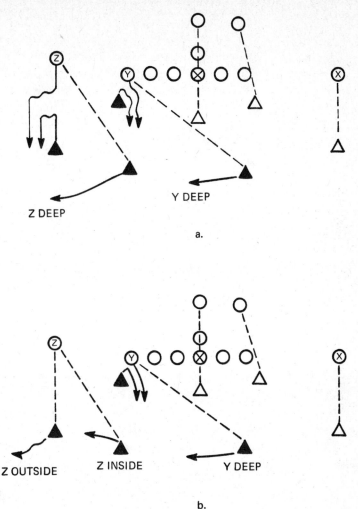

Diagram 10-8

halfback from inside cuts, then glides to the inside ready to pick up the tight end if he breaks out shallow. The strong backer rips the tight end at the line of scrimmage, forcing him to an inside release, then reacts out to pick up the running back wherever he goes.

The strong safety picks up the split back after he clears the strong corner, and the weak-side safety shuffles over to cover the tight end deep. The Mike man moves to the strong side, checking the tight end for the quick pop pass, the hook, the curl, and crossing patterns.

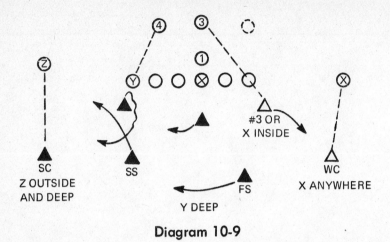

Diagram 10-9

On the weak side the backer is assigned the fullback if he swings to the defensive right. However, if he blocks passer protection, the backer drops off to provide inside coverage on the split end.

Diagram 10-9 illustrates a method of moving the defensive backfield strength on the snap of the ball to meet an offensive overload. The strong corner covers the split back if he breaks out or goes deep. The strong safety plays an invert technique ready to break up the slant-in and pick patterns. If the split back goes deep, he looks for the tight end or the near back in the flat.

The strong backer rips the tight end and obstructs him from outside cuts to a depth of six yards then slides outside, ready to pick up the near back if he breaks deep or outside. The Mike man drops off to the strong side ready to pick up the tight end on a quick inside break or the near back if he runs a circle-in route.

WEAK-SIDE OVERLOAD

Providing an overload to the offensive weak side can be accomplished by the coverage illustrated in Diagram 10-10. This scheme provides double coverage on both weak-side receivers of a pro-spread formation and could be used to advantage whenever weak-side tendencies are indicated or when a weak-side flood pattern may be thrown.

The strong-side safety, corner, and outside backer play their basic responsibilities on the strong side. The weak-side outside backer moves out on the split end playing him "eye-inside" on the

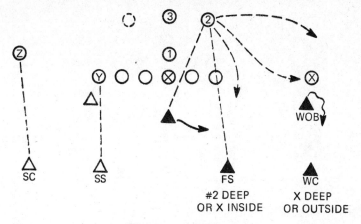

Diagram 10-10

line of scrimmage. He keys the near back, contacts the split end as he releases and drops off with him maintaining inside leverage. If the near back swings or flares to his side, he releases the split end at 3-4 yards to pick up this back in the flat. If the near back blocks or runs a circle route, he continues to provide inside coverage on the split end.

The weak-side corner back keys the split end ready to cover him alone deep if the outside backer must release to the near back, otherwise he will attain an outside position on the end in double coverage.

The free safety keys the near back as usual, taking him on all deep routes. If he blocks or runs a short pattern, the free safety slides over to provide inside-out coverage on the split end.

The middle linebacker also keys the near back, then reacts on the snap of the ball to the weak side, picking up the back on circle patterns or obstructing him from breaking deep. If the near back blocks, he drops off looking for the split end on a break-in or the tight end on a crossing pattern.

COMBINATION FOUR-DEEP MAN-FOR-MAN, AND ZONE COVERAGES

In Chapter 8, I reviewed some of the possibilities for combination coverage wherein the deep backs played zone and the linebackers were employed in a variety of man-for-man assignments.

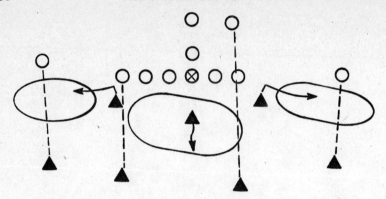

Diagram 10-11

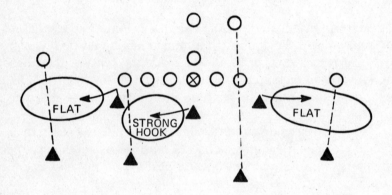

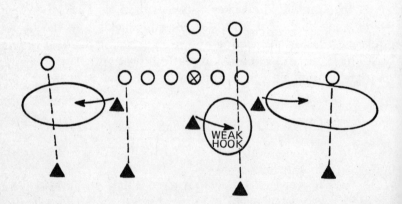

Diagram 10-12

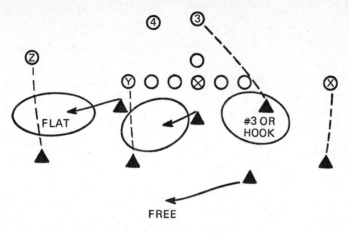

Diagram 10-13

The four-deep man-for-man alignment can likewise be combined with a variety of linebacker zone assignments to provide additional change-ups or to better utilize certain defensive personnel. The basic combination coverage of this type is shown in Diagram 10-11. The four deep backs are playing their usual "man" assignments, while the three linebackers are dropping off to assigned zones. Since this is a balanced coverage, the outside backers are covering their flat zones, and the middle backer is dropping to the short center zone.

This basic coverage can be easily adjusted into an overload toward the strong side or the weak side of the offensive formation by merely assigning the middle backer to the strong or weak hook zones, thereby providing four pass defenders on one side and three on the other (Diagram 10-12).

Another overload to the strong side which can provide a change of pace is illustrated in Diagram 10-13. By assigning the weak-side backer to the running back man-for-man, the combination overload previously illustrated (Diagram 10-12) can be strengthened by the addition of a free safety. This coverage provides maximum strength to the strong side while retaining adequate man-for-man coverage on the weak side.

Many other types of special combination coverages can be devised from the four-deep man-for-man. Diagram 10-14 is a method of double coverage on the split end while still providing a four-man overload to the strong side of the offensive formation. The versatility of the four-deep alignment is again demonstrated by

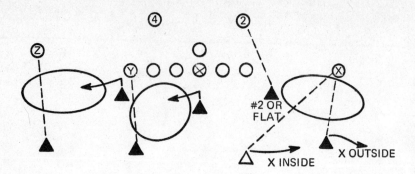

Diagram 10-14

the large number of coverages which are possible from this formation yet demand the application of only basic pass defense techniques.

BLITZING

When the pass defense scheme calls for blitzing to gain a strong rush on the quarterback, close coverage must be applied to the intended receivers. Time is of the essence in attacking a blitzing defense, therefore the quarterback will attempt to hit his receivers quickly before the rushers can drop him. If the defensive backs can stay with the receivers for 10-12 yards, the rushers should be able to get to the passer. This close coverage cannot be accomplished as well with the zone defense, so the man-for-man is preferred when a blitz has been called.

Blitzing is most effective if it can be disguised. It is advisable to incorporate the four-deep zone or a combination with the four-deep man-for-man so that the offensive quarterback cannot anticipate the blitz by reading the containing pass coverage. Individual players must also be cautious about tipping the defensive hand. The free safety, for example, is frequently a good key for the quarterback. If the safety prematurely moves close to the line of scrimmage to better cover the running back or to blitz himself, a favorite automatic is the split-end post pattern (Diagram 10-15).

Those defenders who are usually employed in blitzing can enhance the defense by faking a blitz or by jitterbugging—jumping into the line, shuffling in place, leaning forward as if to gain momentum, then backing out. Such tactics can cause confusion in

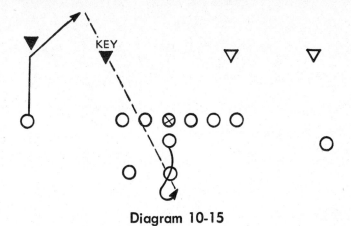

Diagram 10-15

the offensive team by making the blocking assignments uncertain. If a defender can make the offense think he is going to blitz, they may hold in another man or two to block, possibly cutting down on the number of receivers that will be released, or disrupting the offensive flare control.

Blitzing and stunting can be valuable adjuncts to the overall defense if they are used with discretion. Besides increasing the pass rush, these tactics can also be used to protect the wide side of the field, adjust to a strong formation or to an obvious tendency. Only those blitzes or stunts that have a specific purpose should be included in the plans for a particular game and their purposes should be fully understood by all defensive personnel.

RUN-REACTION IN THE FOUR-DEEP

It is generally conceded that a man-for-man defense will react to the running game faster than a zone type defense. The defender in the "man" defense generally has a more positive key for determining run or pass and his run-reaction responsibilities can be more easily defined. The four-deep man-for-man, however, can present some definite weaknesses in outside run protection unless the pass defense unit is well trained in defending this particular phase of the running game. If the outside backer, the corner back, and the safety are well coordinated, read their keys properly, and react and support aggressively, the end sweeps and off-tackle plays can be contained as effectively from the man as from the zone.

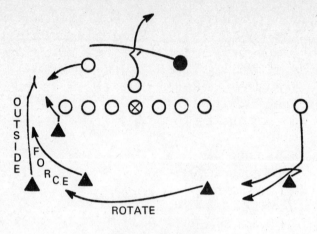

Diagram 10-16

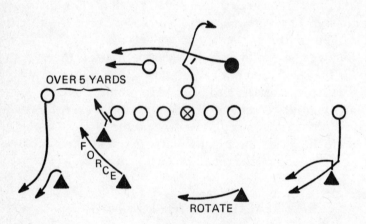

Diagram 10-17

On a tight formation side the corner back must assume the outside run responsibility, while the outside backer and safety provide an inside-out force (Diagram 10-16).

On the side of a split halfback or split end the distance the split man is removed from the formation determines who has the outside responsibility. If the split man is beyond five yards, the safety must assume this responsibility and he accomplishes it with an inside-out force (Diagram 10-17). The split man in many offenses will be used to drive the corner back deep thus delaying his run-reaction. The safety's assigned man will generally be required as a blocker on runs to his side thus providing the safety with an immediate reaction key.

Each safety man should be responsible for indicating who has force responsibility on his respective side of the field unless a line or backfield stunt has been called which already indicates that responsibility.

As a running play develops, the "off" side safety rotates first to the deep center area then supports the force man. The "off" side corner back likewise rotates toward the play. However, if the split receiver on his side has released downfield, he must check him and maintain an inside relationship being ready for the throwback.

Chapter 11

SPECIAL PROBLEMS IN
PASS DEFENSE

Some consideration must be given to the special situations that may confront the pass defense unit. Sometimes these conditions are beyond our control, such as the weather, and sometimes they are special aspects of the game that can be anticipated and prepared for in advance. The greater the detailed preparation that a coaching staff can attain, the greater are the chances for success during the season.

WEATHER AND FIELD CONDITIONS

Prior to entering an opponent's dressing room, I make it a practice to walk the members of my team out to the playing field to examine its condition. We make mental notes, particularly of soft areas on the field that may be the result of poor drainage, over-watering, or faulty sprinkler heads. These are danger areas for the pass defender and can adversely affect his footing during coverage. It is difficult to cut on a wet field so it is advisable to cover a receiver more loosely in these areas.

A wet field assists the pass rush because it is difficult for the blockers to set their back feet. A direct, straight ahead pass rush is most effective against the retreating cup defenders on a wet field. Rushers should carry their body weight well forward and keep their hands in front of them, slapping, pushing, grabbing and throwing the blockers from their path.

In the defensive secondary it is advisable to use a zone coverage in wet weather. The offensive receiver has the advantage

on a wet field since he knows where he is going. It is difficult to cut
sharply in running precision pass patterns on a soggy turf, but it is
even more difficult to cover those cuts. In a man-for-man defense
the defender must make an immediate reaction to the receiver. As
the receiver makes his moves, the defender must make corresponding moves—not so in the zone. The zone defender plays more
loosely. His reaction is to the ball so he need not "mirror image"
the receiver, meaning he will have less possibility of slipping or
losing his relationship with the receiver. Then, too, the zone defender has the advantage of more interception possibilities in wet
weather. The quarterback will have difficulty planting his back foot
for body power in deep throws, consequently he must resort to
more arm action. This reduces the usual distance of his throws and
makes them more erratic. Since his blockers are having greater
difficulty protecting him, his throws are necessarily hurried. All of
these factors add up to the possibility of interception if the defenders are keying the football and reacting to it properly.

DEFENDING AGAINST PLAY-ACTION PASSES

Any complete pass offense will have its share of play-action
passes and if the offense has established a strong running game,
these can be some of the most dangerous passes in their repertoire.

Play action can serve a number of purposes. Inside fakes can
slow down and virtually eliminate a hard rush by the defensive
ends. Sometimes play action is designed to freeze or draw a
linebacker, making it possible to throw in his area, and since the
quarterback sets up to throw from different spots in play action, the
effectiveness of the pass rush is reduced.

Instant recognition is the key to playing good pass defense
against a play-action attack. All personnel must be thoroughly acquainted with the opponent's play patterns and recognize them
immediately so they are not delayed or drawn out of position, even
momentarily.

The opponent's play-action passes must be identified from
scouting reports and film analysis. Diagram these plays to include
each offensive assignment on charts and display them in the team
dressing room the week of the game. Set up your defensive backfield on the practice field and walk an offensive unit through each
play until your personnel become familiar with them. Point out the
distinctions between the opponent's actual running play and its

corresponding play-action pass. Indicate any keys that will assist in an immediate recognition of a run or pass.

Next, let the defense see the play at normal speeds. Have your defensive backs take their positions on the field and review each of their assignments as an offensive unit runs through each of the opponent's favorite patterns. Finally allocate ten or 15 minutes of practice time on Tuesday and Wednesday to a full speed pass defense scrimmage in which the accompanying running plays are interspersed with the play-action passes.

If a film of the next opponent is available, it should be reviewed on Monday to introduce your defensive unit to the nature of their pass offense. Show the film again on Thursday after your defensive preparations have been made so that each player can visualize how he will react to each play-action situation.

Scout reports should indicate when play-action type passes are most frequently employed by an opponent. Each team has tendencies and by knowing these tendencies the defensive backs can anticipate specific offensive tactics and be ready for them.

The coverage of play-action passes need not be any different from that employed on other passes, except that the defensive outside rushers may be committed to run-protection if the offensive faking is done well. If the defensive ends are sometimes assigned to a flat zone or to a specific offensive man, some adjustment may be advisable in the overall pass defense if the play-action run threats are directed consistently at the ends.

SPRINT-OUT PASSES

When the ball passes the offensive tackles as it does in sprint-out, roll-out, and halfback running pass plays, new problems are created for the pass defense unit. As long as the quarterback and the ball stay inside the tackles, there is no running threat to the flat zone protectors so normal pass coverages can be used. Those pass offenses wherein the quarterback merely rolls up behind the tackles create no new problems to the pass coverage defenders. This pass system is designed to present problems to the rushers since the protective cup is moving—sometimes behind one tackle, then the other, and occasionally behind the center.

But the running pass plays that threaten to develop into sweeps call for special preparation of the defensive unit.

The sprint-out pass and all of its variations have become

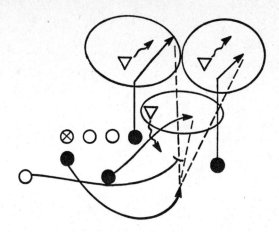

Diagram 11-1

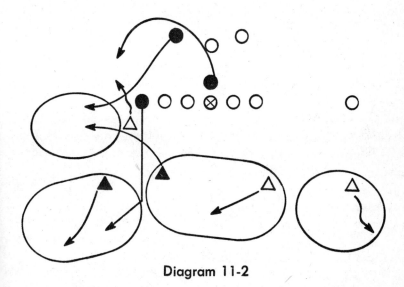

Diagram 11-2

very popular in recent years and are difficult to cover (Diagram 11-1). I believe in the use of several coverages against those teams that feature this type of offense.

Against tight formation teams such as a wishbone the invert defense will be very effective (Diagram 11-2). The invert backs key the quarterback and move with the ball. As the outside halfback flares into the flat, the invert back slides out with him in coverage and the defensive end provides an inside-out force on the quarterback. The off-side defensive end should check for a reverse then drop off to assist in protecting against a throw back.

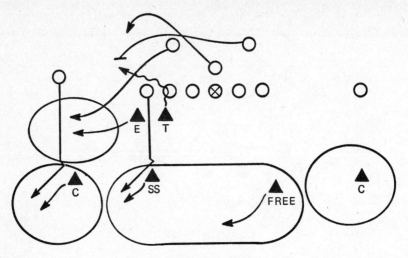

Diagram 11-3

Against teams that use wide-set flankers and split ends, however, the invert defense is not advisable, so other tactics must be employed.

The split-end side of most offenses does not create the sprint-out pass problems that exist on the tight-end side. Unless a slot back is used toward the split end it is difficult to get a three-man flood such as can be generated on the tight-end side.

I like to use four different types of coverages against the sprint-out toward the tight-end side. By doing this the offense will not know who will cover the particular receivers and we can present an element of surprise. Three of these coverages are from a zone and the other is a man-for-man coverage.

In Diagram 11-3, our end drops off to the flat zone and we contain with the tackle. This coverage leaves the weak-side safety free to provide deep protection on the strong half of the field.

When strong tendencies indicate a sprint-out pass, the strong-side safety can move up to a rover position and provide flat coverage as we adjust into a three-deep zone (Diagram 11-4).

A coverage which is provided on key is our rotation from a four-deep zone. On pass situations all four deep backs key the quarterback. As he begins his sprint-out pass action the onside corner comes up to attack the split receiver and then covers the flat zone. The onside safety moves over to cover deep outside and the offside safety shifts to the deep center zone (Diagram 11-5).

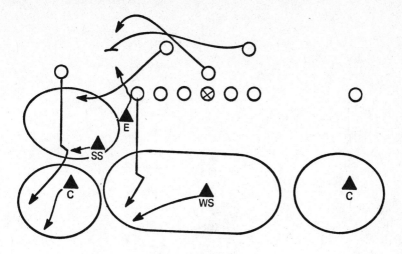

Diagram 11-4

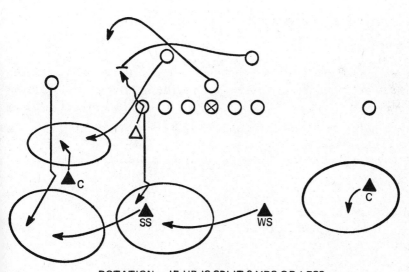

ROTATION — IF HB IS SPLIT 6 YDS OR LESS

Diagram 11-5

Our man-for-man coverage is standard and is usually employed inside our ten-yard line. A frequently used change-up is to
force the quarterback with the weak-side linebacker on sprint-outs
to his side, while full responsibility for the running back is assumed
by the free safety (Diagram 11-6).

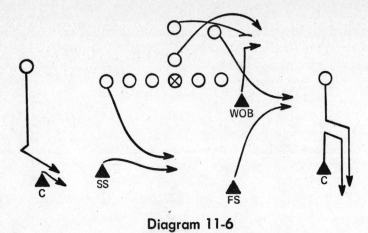

Diagram 11-6

GOAL LINE PASS DEFENSE

Tight coverage is required in the goal line situation and that requirement can only be met with a man-for-man coverage system. There can be no cushion allowed between the receiver and the defensive back since passes in this area are necessarily short quick passes.

The man-for-man defense will assure that no one is wasted covering an area which is not threatened. Every defensive back is assigned to an offensive receiver and if a receiver stays in to block as a part of the passer protection cup, that defender who is assigned to that man will now provide a double coverage on an adjacent receiver.

An extra advantage of the man-for-man is the opportunity it affords to assign the best defender to the best receiver. Scouting reports frequently indicate a favorite pass pattern or a favorite receiver used inside the ten-yard line.

Proper alignment is especially important in this area since the slightest defensive error can result in a quick touchdown. Depth is the first consideration. Since the pass area becomes smaller as the offense gets closer to the goal line, the defensive backs should adjust their depth accordingly. At the ten-yard line they may play a normal man-for-man distance away from their receiver. At the five-yard line that distance should be halved, while at the one- or two-yard line the defender will be standing on the goal line. At no time in a standard man-for-man defense should a defender take a position five or six yards in the end zone. This closeness to the line of scrimmage also assists the defense of the running game and as a receiver blocks for a run, his assigned defender can immediately react by filling the hole.

Simplicity should be the key word in establishing a goal line defense. Multiple assignments should be held to an absolute minimum. All backs should key only on the men to whom they are assigned. Switching of assignments on crossing patterns should only be done if a block or pick situation develops. On any switch there is necessarily a moment when both receivers are open until the defenders can again close up on them.

Scouting reports and film analysis should indicate the favorite pass receivers and their favorite pass routes at the goal line. In taking their positions in the man-for-man the defensive backs should align themselves laterally to take away each receiver's favorite routes. One should never take a head-up position on the receiver since this allows him equal opportunity to break in or out.

Against a pro-spread formation the corner backs are assigned to the first eligible receiver in from their sideline. The safeties are assigned to the second receivers in from their respective near sidelines. Outside linebackers are assigned to the near running back on their side if he releases to their side (Diagram 11-7).

If an offensive formation has no wide receiver outside the tight end, the corner back and adjacent safety switch their usual man-for-man assignments (Diagram 11-8). The corner back now picks up the near back (the second man from the sideline) and the safety takes the tight end (first man in from the sideline). This switch of assignments allows the corner back to stay wide where he can maintain an outside leverage on sweep plays.

Many teams use man-in-motion plays at the goal line even though they may seldom use this action in the middle of the playing field. The intention is usually four-fold: to draw an offside penalty from an anxious defensive lineman; to distract attention from the point of attack; to create an overload situation; or to draw a defender from an area, then attack that area.

A man-in-motion should never draw a linebacker out of his position. Adjustments to a man-in-motion should always come from the defensive backs. I believe that it is vital to leave the linemen and inside linebackers undisturbed in the goal-line defense. Their primary responsibility is the run and all their efforts should be

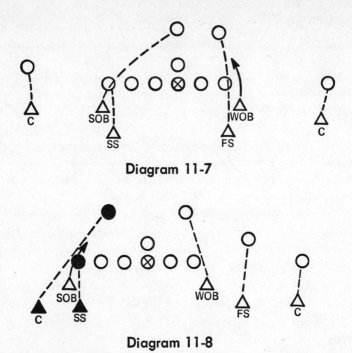

Diagram 11-7

Diagram 11-8

geared to that assignment since even inches may determine success or failure in this field area.

Passes in this area are necessarily short, quick passes. The corner backs should align themselves on split receivers to take away the slant-in pass and force the receiver to the outside. Good use of the bump-and-run technique can be made in this area and the delay of receivers will assist the linemen in getting to the quarterback. When the receiver breaks outside, the defender should play him tight and move in front of him watching his eyes. If the ball is not thrown immediately, one should be ready for the "up" pattern. Now the old rule of "never let the receiver get behind you" does not apply. As the receiver breaks up field the defender should maintain a tight relationship with him but *between* him and the quarterback. Having prevented the quick pass, the defender now wants to force the quarterback to attempt to throw a high, soft pass over the defender. The defender's position is such that he should be able to make a high point interception on such a ball. The defender in goal line defense must play for the ball when it is thrown—there is no point in tackling the receiver *after* the pass has been completed. To play for the ball the defender must be in front of the receiver or in a position where he can quickly move

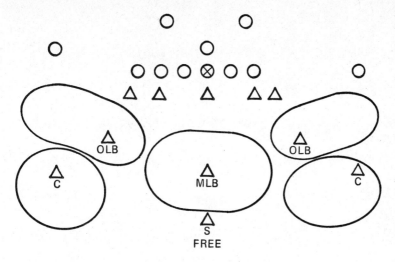

Diagram 11-9

in front of the receiver when the ball is thrown. At the goal line, safeties and corner backs must play pass defense like linebackers—always ready to take the interception route.

PREVENT DEFENSES

Several game situations suggest the use of a loose type of pass defense which concentrates on preventing a long gain or a touchdown. The obvious pass situation, third down and extremely long yardage, or being ahead late in either half of a game are situations in which the use of a "prevent" type of defense may be advisable.

This type of defense must emphasize maximum pass coverage and as a result will sacrifice the rush and delay aspects of total team pass defense. A loose zone alignment which provides strong deep coverage is generally utilized and a favorite over the years has been the 5-3-2-1 with the backs and linebackers merely taking deeper and wider positions than normal. Some coaches have dropped the middle linebacker to a depth of 6-8 yards so that they can in turn move the safety back to 15-18 yards and let him play center-field (Diagram 11-9).

In this alignment the defensive ends can cover the flats or they can provide a strong outside rush on the quarterback and give away the flats. The middle guard can be responsible for draw plays and the center screen pass, while the tackles coordinate their charge with the play of the defensive ends.

Some coaches have completely abandoned the use of a special defense for "prevent" situations. They have had too many bad experiences with opponents well drilled in the two-minute offense. Most prevent defenses are vulnerable to hook, curl, and sideline patterns, and if the offense is well schooled in the art of using the clock, they can easily march the length of the field in 60 seconds using these patterns. Then, too, since the secondary defenders are spread out, they cannot support each other as in a normal defense and one error, slip, or missed tackle following a completed pass can result in a quick score.

Some coaches merely loosen up their basic defenses to meet prevent situations. They feel that their players are already familiar with these defenses and there is nothing new to teach. The players have confidence in these defenses and they must be pretty good, otherwise how did their opponent get into his long-yardage situation in the first place?

A defense which can avoid most of the weaknesses of traditional "prevents" is the combination man-for-man, two-deep zone. This defense provides man coverage on all receivers—making the sideline, curl, and hook patterns less effective—and yet affords two center fielders to provide double coverage insurance on receivers who break deep.

This defense can be executed from the pro-43 or the old Eagle 52 alignment (Diagram 11-10). I am partial to the Eagle alignment since both inside linebackers can move to the outside where they can cover the usual running back patterns more easily.

In the Eagle, the middle guard is again assigned draw and center screen pass responsibility. The tackles take positions in which they can direct their charges at an inward angle through the offensive guards' outside shoulder, pinching him to the inside. The initial combined charge of the tackles and the middle guard will seal off the inside against a running play, then as a pass shows, they can re-direct their momentum to the quarterback. The defensive end on the split-end side is free to put an outside rush on the quarterback. The strong-side defensive end should step into the tight end, delaying him with a blow while keying the near back ready to cover him man-for-man if he releases to his side. This blow will also protect the strong-side linebacker from the tight end

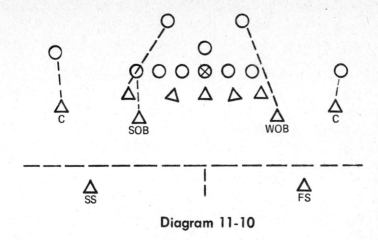

Diagram 11-10

block if an off-tackle play develops. The delay of the tight end makes it relatively easy now for the linebacker to pick him up man-for-man if a pass develops.

The corner backs must position themselves to deny quick inside routes, forcing the receivers into outside releases.

The free safeties will align themselves approximately 12-14 yards deep and split the two receivers to their respective sides. Each is responsible for one-half of the field. They key the quarterback and the ball and stay behind the deepest receiver on their side of the field. These should be the fastest and best zone defense ball hawks on the team, and since every receiver already has a defender assigned man-for-man these two men are actually providing a double coverage on the deepest receivers—and that is what the prevent defense is for—to prevent the deep pass!

Chapter 12

GAME PREPARATION OF
THE PASS DEFENSE

The test of the pudding is in the taste, and the test of one's pass defense is in the game. How effectively a coach brings all of his accumulated football knowledge to bear on the preparation of his team for a successful game is the true test of his ability.

Planning and preparation are the keys to having a productive week of practices and subsequent victory on the playing field. Here is the point that separates most successful coaches from the unsuccessful ones. The planning for next week's contest must begin as soon as this week's contest is over. During the weekend the players and fans can dwell on the success or failure of the game just finished, reminisce about the good and the bad, savoring the thrill of victory or languishing in the dejection of defeat, but the good coaching staff goes to work.

As soon as the dressing room is clear after a contest, the coaches should meet briefly for the head coach to outline his general thoughts about the next opponent. At this time he should present his estimate of their strengths and weaknesses and suggest tentative strategies. Each staff member has his assigned duties to perform during the weekend of planning—phases of scouting report analysis, statistics and charts analysis, film analysis—and the head coach should specify any other special tasks or assignments that he wants accomplished before the staff holds its general weekend meeting. There is a lot of work to be done, decisions to be made and plans to be laid. The successful staff devotes many hours to these tasks and begins the next week's practice with definite goals and detailed plans to achieve them. The unsuccessful staff is usually inadequate in its planning and preparation, sometimes fails to develop a plan before the new week of practice begins and consequently wastes a day or two of vital practice while members coach "off the cuff."

ALLOCATION OF PRACTICE TIME

The defensive coordinator generally has to be sold on the need for adequate practice time for the development of all phases of pass defense. There is a tendency among most defensive coaches to think too heavily about defending the running game. Offensively, I'm sure that most coaches would agree that a sound running game must be established before a good pass offense can be developed. Conversely then, it follows that on defense one must first be able to neutralize the running game to then be successful against the passing game. Unfortunately, too many coaches get so involved with elaborate plans and techniques to defend the run that pass defense gets only token consideration. Those coaches responsible for developing phases of the pass defense scheme must be prepared to present their case at staff meetings when the allocations of practice time are made.

As I have stated in Chapter 1, if your opponent is hitting a 50-50 ratio of run and pass in his offense, then it behooves the defensive coaching staff to achieve a 50-50 ratio of run and pass defensive preparation time to get ready for them.

PRELIMINARY PLANNING

As most coaches do, I keep a file of scouting reports on teams I have played. Going back over an opponent's old scouting reports from previous seasons is my first step in preparing for them. I am reminded of plays and formations that have been successful for them in the past, I note any trick plays that they have used previously, and I can recognize favorite pass patterns used year after year.

However, in addition to the old scouting reports in these files I also include each year's accumulation of newspaper articles on each team, programs, and player rosters. From an examination of these I can determine the number of starters graduated from last year's team, and by comparing with current rosters I can identify new personnel and shifts of player positions. Such an analysis can suggest potential weaknesses or strengths to be examined more thoroughly when reviewing current scouting reports and game films.

In each team's file I also place our post-game observations in which our players and staff have evaluated our preparation, game plan, and execution. Accompanying this information are copies of the practice plans for the week preceding the game. A quick review of these papers provides more ideas on how to approach our preparation for this opponent this season. Some drills we devised last year may have been very effective and should be repeated. Perhaps we did not allot enough practice time for the development of certain individual or unit techniques. Maybe last year's preparation was ideal and the format should be used again.

Finally, I review the film of our game played against this opponent last year. I glance at the film analysis report that was made by our staff, but primarily I run through the film rather quickly just to familiarize myself with their team, the game, their strategy, and oft-repeated pass patterns.

This preliminary work has now set the stage for a review of all that information which we have accumulated on this opponent this year. With this background material we can now analyze our opponent's personnel and current offense in the light of what has been successful for them in the past. We can compare strengths and weaknesses and attain a greater depth of understanding of the strategies and philosophies of the opposing coaching staff. The more you know about your opponent, the better you can defend against him.

UTILIZATION OF THE SCOUTING REPORT

I have seen dozens of types of defensive scouting reports from various sections of the United States. Some are very simple, merely outlining favorite formations and plays with an evaluation of personnel and a player roster attached. Others are one-half inch in thickness, so complicated it took four scouts to compile, and filled with minutiae and trivia that contribute little or nothing to game preparation.

In my opinion, a defensive scouting report should be simple, concise, and factual. I want a report that will give general information on the team, such as formations and patterns, down and distance and field position tendencies, and pertinent facts about key personnel.

A key portion of the report is the tendency section. All teams have tendencies, but they may not show themselves in any particular game. The breaks of a game, the rhythm of the game, or a weak or strong opponent may break a team from its normal tendencies. For this reason it is unwise to develop a game plan and a week of preparation based on one scouting report. The summaries of two reports may be more valid, but I believe that one must scout an opponent at least three times to gain an adequate picture of his tendencies. Ideally, I would like to have a report on every game that every one of my conference foes has played prior to our meeting. One cannot defend against everything that an opponent's offense can throw at your team; your best bet is to determine what they do best, determine when they do it and set your defenses accordingly.

EVALUATING FORMATIONS

My first concern is the favorite formations of the opponent. In this day of wide-open offenses, even high school teams may use ten or 20 different formations during a single game. But with which ones are they really playing football? Tendencies of these multiple offense teams in three games will usually indicate that their most effective plays are developing from only three or four formations. These, then, are the formations for which your defenses need to be adjusted and your players prepared to meet. I'm not saying that you should disregard the other formations but I am saying that these should receive the *bulk* of your preparation time.

A good defensive coach must be well schooled in offense. As the consolidated scouting reports identify the opponent's favorite formations, the defensive coach should recognize the offensive potential of those formations, the strengths and weaknesses. Is the opponent really exploiting the formation or is he only doing certain things from it?

One of the best drop-back pass offenses is the pro-spread with split backs (Diagram 12-1). One of its advantages is that one or both running backs can quickly release into a pattern. If scouting reports indicate that the opponent seldom or never throws to backs releasing from the backfield, then he is not getting the full poten-

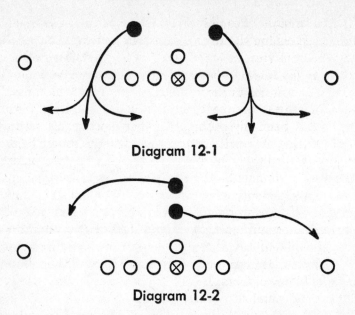

Diagram 12-1

Diagram 12-2

tial of this formation. Since this is not a strong inside-tackle running formation (the fullback position is vacant) there are many implications for successfully defending under these circumstances.

Diagram 12-2 illustrates a Pro-I formation. For a team that emphasizes the drop-back pass this is one of the least effective formations. Neither running back can get into a downfield pass pattern quickly. Swing passes and screen passes are about the only patterns which these backs can run effectively, unless motion is used. Again, there are many implications for successfully adjusting one's defenses to meet a drop-back pass team using a Pro-I. The formation is strong for running, but the pass defense problems are simplified.

Every offensive formation is designed to facilitate certain types of runs and certain types of passes. Each should be analyzed in the light of what your opponent is doing from that formation and how you can best defend against it.

IDENTIFYING FAVORITE PASS PATTERNS

There are many different methods of developing pass of fenses. Some teams use a limited number of set patterns that are rehearsed like their running plays. They may have one set for zon coverage and another for man-for-man coverage. Another tear may have very few team-type coordinated patterns, but an almo:

unlimited number of combinations which can be developed by the quarterback calling the route of the primary receiver, while adjacent receivers run various coordinated routes which are predetermined by rules. In between these two extremes, there are as many other systems as there are pass-offense-oriented coaches.

Regardless of what system is being used by a particular team, it has been my observation that most teams settle into a definite catalog of favorite patterns and favorite routes by the time they have played their third game of the season. Two factors influence this development—the abilities of the quarterback and his receivers and the successes that they have achieved in these early contests. What has worked satisfactorily in previous games is what the quarterback and coaching staff will tend to rely on in their next game. The difficult teams to prepare for are those that have tried a great many things in the early season and haven't been particularly successful in any of them. It is difficult to predict what they may do in their next game!

One of the most difficult tasks for a two-man scouting team is to record accurately the routes of all pass receivers on every pass play. We ask that they at least record the route of the man to whom the ball was thrown, then diagram as many other routes as they can determine, *but do not guess*. From the formation and the primary receiver's route we can generally identify the total pattern from previous scouting reports, records of previous years, or opponent game films that we receive in exchange.

Having identified ten or 12 of the opponent's favorite and most successful patterns, we can now set them up on paper against our own defenses to determine what if any adjustments may be necessary in our coverage to give us additional advantage. Where are they *not* throwing? This information can suggest a sacrifice of coverage in one area to strengthen another area.

IDENTIFYING FAVORITE RECEIVERS AND THEIR ROUTES

The identification of an opponent's favorite receivers is no problem. The statisticians and newspaper reporters will do this. The pass defense coach is interested in what each receiver's favorite routes are. Receivers are like any other player—they have some things they do well and some things they do not do so well. In our preparation we want to identify these things. If we can cover a receiver's good routes, we can force him into his not so good routes—this should increase our interception possibilities.

The capabilities of some receivers may dictate a shift of our defensive personnel. If it will not create too many other problems, we may want to shift personnel to have our best defender in a position where he will most generally be covering their best receiver.

Those several routes that are favored by each receiver become the routes which each defender will concentrate on in practice as we prepare for this opponent. Extra practice time will be devoted to individual and unit coverage of these routes. Special emphasis should be put on identifying these routes as they unfold.

Information from scouting reports should not only tell you in what areas or zones your opponent is not throwing, but should also tell you to which receivers they are seldom if ever throwing. Again, this becomes valuable information in determining your placement of personnel or in adjusting your defenses to particular sets or situations. If you can identify their worst receiver, you can concentrate on their best receiver.

ANALYZING TENDENCIES

For many years I have used a simple scouting form for the accumulation of tendencies (Diagram 12-3). Actually, one person can easily chart every offensive play in a game using this form. If both teams playing are future opponents, we chart them both at the same time. It is better of course to have two men scouting, then one can chart the opponent's defenses and call off the down and distance for the man recording offensive tendencies.

Besides recording down, distance and field position for every play, we are especially interested in the offensive formation, backfield play pattern, and pass routes, particularly the receiver to whom the ball was thrown. We are only casually interested in blocking assignments since we feel we can determine these from our analysis of the opponent's game films. If we can record the above information for three games, it is felt that definite tendencies will be indicated. Most good college offensive teams today will average between 60 and 70 plays per game. Tendencies noted for three games then are the result of observing 180–210 offensive plays and should have fair validity.

From the standpoint of pass defense preparation, our first interest is formation tendencies. What are their two or three favorite passing formations? These are the ones for which we want to be

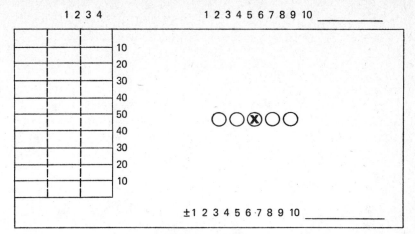

Diagram 12-3

1. Indicate down by circling number 1-4 in upper left of each chart.

2. Indicate yardage to be gained by circling number 1-10 at top of each chart.

3. Indicate with an "×" the pre-snap ball position on the field diagram.

4. Complete offensive formation and chart movements of key personnel on each play.

5. Indicate yardage gained or lost by circling the "+" or "−" and the appropriate number (1-10) at the bottom of the chart. If yardage is greater than 10 yards, write in space provided.

particularly prepared. These are the ones for which we will make whatever special basic adjustments may be necessary in our standard defensive alignments. All adjustments to other offensive formations or sets that the opponent may use must flow from these foundations.

Our next task is to establish the five or six most frequently used pass patterns run from each of the favorite formations. These, of course, are drawn up in detail and included in the scouting report distributed to the players at the Monday pre-practice squad meeting.

Also, from each favorite formation we chart the route of the receiver or would-be receiver of *every* pass thrown from that formation. This summary chart might look similar to the example in Diagram 12-4. At a glance, one can see who the favorite receivers are in a particular formation and what routes they are running.

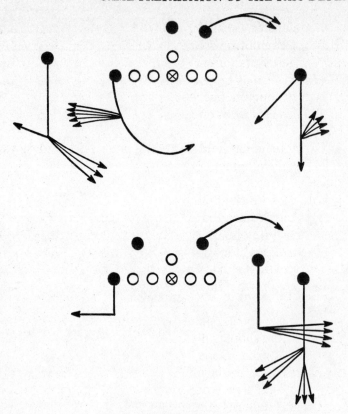

Diagram 12-4

Analysis of the opponent's hash-mark offense is our next concern. Since about two-thirds of their offensive plays will start on or near a hash-mark, it is advantageous to determine what their tendencies are from this position. Many interesting characteristics show up from this analysis and I am always amazed that some coaches are so unaware of their tendencies. I have seen teams that never run into the sideline, sprintout pass teams that never sprint out to the sideline, and teams that throw their flood patterns only to the open side of the field. But many other things will surface of which advantage can be taken by the pass defense coach. Some teams never throw their swing passes or screen passes to the near sideline. Some quarterbacks who use the rolling "behind the tackle" passer protection cups never roll toward the sideline from a hash-mark. This tendency of course has some strong implications for the defensive coordinator in divising his pass rush strategies.

If tendencies from the hash-mark can be determined tha

allow the defensive backfield coach to place less emphasis on certain patterns or routes, concentration can be made on the more dangerous ones. Rotations or stunts away from the sideline and into double coverages may be possible. The coach has to weigh the odds in playing tendencies, but when two teams are evenly matched, the one that has the odds on its side will win. That's how Las Vegas was built!

Every team has field position tendencies based on yard line position. The development of these tendencies begins with the first discussion of strategy a coach has with his offensive quarterback and is fortified with the field position chart that is usually a part of every quarterback's handbook. But of particular significance to pass defense is the type of pass pattern used at either end of the field. Other tendencies will have to indicate what patterns an opponent will use between the 20-yard lines; but the field position chart should indicate on what he relies to get out of trouble or to get into the end zone.

Are there special patterns used in these areas? Inside the ten-yard lines, he should anticipate a man-for-man defense and run appropriate patterns. Does he? Here again we want to identify those patterns that are favorites in these areas. These should be included in the players' scout report and will become a major part of the goal line defense preparation.

Down and distance tendencies show considerable variation from one team to another. As pass offenses get more adept and more consistent, more teams are throwing on first down. A good quarterback wants to gain at least five yards on first down. If he is capable and confident, he may not hesitate to throw at this time. Those teams with erratic pass offenses, however, may never throw on first down—a factor of considerable advantage to the defense, since with this tendency indicated, the defense can now overload for the run and make the quarterback's job that much more difficult.

I break down and distance tendencies into the following categories:

First down and 10 yards to go—These will be the opponent's best and most consistent normal yardage plays.

First down and more than 10 yards to go—Will they go to the air immediately or wait until second or third down?

Second down and normal yardage (from 4 to 7 yards)—Like first and ten they will use their best and most consistent plays.

Second down and long yardage (more than seven yards)—Pass or run?

Second down and short yardage (less than four yards)—To some teams this is a down for throwing the deep pass, having confidence that their running game can still gain the first down on the next play if needed.

Third or fourth down and normal yardage (three yards or less)—Here the opponent will normally use his best power plays or most consistent short-yardage passes.

Third or fourth down and long yardage (more than three yards)—Pass situations for most teams.

Within each of these categories we are interested first in determining what they do most frequently: pass or run. What is the ratio? Diagram 12-5 is an illustration of the down and distance tendencies of two contrasting opponents in a recent season.

The next task is to diagram the three or four favorite running plays and three or four favorite pass plays in each category. These plays become the main portion of our opponent's offense for which we will prepare our defensive team during the week's practice. These are the plays that we must stop. Again, this information is illustrated in the scouting report summary distributed to all of our players for study. These plays should be anticipated in these down and distance game situations and the appropriate defensive calls made to meet them.

Too frequently, coaches get bogged down in the utilization of their scouting report by covering too many details. Only so much material can be presented to a team in its weekly preparation before a point of diminishing returns is reached. There is no point in attempting to prepare a team for everything their opponent *may* do! There is not time for such detailed preparation, nor is it necessary. One must play the odds in preparing for an opponent Napoleon had similar observations when he wrote about preparing his army for battle, "In everything that is undertaken, two-thirds must be calculated, and one-third left to chance. To increase the first fraction would be pusillanimous; to augment the second would be timorous."

TEAM A (2 Games)	TEAM B (2 Games)
Pass-Oriented Team	Run-Oriented
1st—10 (68 X) 52 Runs 16 Passes	1st—10 (52X) 51 Runs 1 Pass
1st and more than 10 (8 X) 2 Runs 6 Passes	1st and more than 10 (4 X) 3 Runs 1 Pass
2nd and normal (18 X) 9 Runs 9 Passes	2nd and normal (10 X) 19 Runs 0 Passes
2nd and long (26 X) 12 Runs 14 Passes	2nd and long (22 X) 16 Runs 6 Passes
2nd and short (18 X) 12 Runs 6 Passes	2nd and short (15 X) 13 Runs 2 Passes
3rd—4th and normal (22 X) 15 Runs 7 Passes	3rd—4th and normal (28 X) 23 Runs 5 Passes
3rd—4th and long (27 X) 6 Runs 21 Passes	3rd—4th and long (16 X) 2 Runs 14 Passes

Diagram 12-5

ANALYZING THE QUARTERBACK

Any personnel analysis of a pass offense must start with the quarterback, and any defensive analysis of a quarterback must be done from two standpoints: how to rush him and how to cover him.

The best pass defense is a strong pass rush. Of prime concern, then, in game preparation is devising the plan for containing the quarterback and putting maximum pressure on him. Generally, the better the passer, the stronger the rush. The reason is quite simple—the better the passer, the greater the chances of his hitting a receiver if given adequate time. If the passer is erratic, one may want to concentrate on coverage and play for the interception.

Is the opponent's quarterback a classic drop-back thrower? Does he have the height to see adequately and throw over rushers? When his protection breaks down, can he scramble? Does he "bail-out" early or does he have the courage to wait for his receivers to break? If he scrambles, does he favor his right side or his left? How quickly does he set up and throw? Most offensive coaches expect their quarterback to deliver the ball within 3.5 seconds after the snap. When scouting an opponent time him with a stop-watch on several plays during the game.

Finally, does the quarterback give any tips that may be of advantage to the rushing unit? Besides tendencies, does he have any habits that may indicate a pass rather than a run? Quarterbacks calling individual routes expend more time in the huddle to call pass plays than running plays. Some quarterbacks unconsciously use a different foot position under the center when they are going to drop back. Some sprint-out quarterbacks alternate their foot position depending on whether they intend to sprint to their right or their left. There are dozens of subtle tips like these that a good scouting team may pick up or that good film analysis may reveal. The pass rush scheme can be enhanced immeasurable with such information.

The most difficult quarterback to cover is the one who sets up quickly, scans his field, fakes with his eyes as well as the ball, and has a quick release. The pros are looking for him—and there are very few. Most quarterbacks have flaws, and in preparing adequate coverage these flaws need to be identified so advantage can be taken of them. Probably the most common bad habit of quarterbacks is the tendency to watch the primary receiver throughout his route. This simplifies pass coverage. If a zone is being used, the defender on the primary receiver can close his cushion and play the man more tightly while other defenders loosen up on their receivers.

Quarterbacks with slow releases tend to telegraph their throws. A common habit is to drop the ball down to waist level in the throwing motion.

Zone defenders may be trained to read this throwing motion and anticipate the ball allowing them a better opportunity for interception.

ANALYZING THE RECEIVERS

Any good pass offense team today must have at least three good receivers. Of these three receivers one of the most important is the tight end. I do not think I can recall a single outstanding pass-oriented football team at any level in recent years that did not have an outstanding tight end. He must be a strong blocker to make the off-tackle running play work, he must be capable of responsibilities in cup protection when needed, but particularly he must be a capable receiver. Without the threat of a tight end the defensive backfield can easily adjust to double coverage on the wide receivers and shut down the pass offense. If the tight end is capable, he poses a constant threat particularly in the middle zones, forcing the safeties and the middle zone under-coverage to stay home.

In my evaluation of receivers in pass defense preparation, I always start with the tight end. His abilities will determine what we can give or take from coverage in his area. This in turn determines the number of possible combinations we have to cover the other receivers.

My next consideration is their worst receiver. How much gambling in coverage can we do with him? For instance, can we afford to single-cover him with a linebacker on critical pass situations to gain double coverage on their favorite receiver with our best defenders?

Finally, we study their favorite receiver. What are his favorite routes that we must stop? What does he do best? The answers to these questions will determine how we take position on him—inside or out, close or loose—whether we zone him or play man for man, when, where, and how we will double-cover him. Naturally we are also concerned about his speed, his height, his jumping ability, and the manner in which he runs his patterns. The defensive backfield coach and his players will study films of him and rehearse coverage techniques over and over during the week of preparation.

DEVELOPING THE RUSHING PLAN

The ability of the opposing passer is the first consideration in deciding on the type of rush to use. If he is fast, quick, and shifty, care must be taken to keep an outside leverage on him. If he is slow, one can gamble more on the outside rush. If the passer can

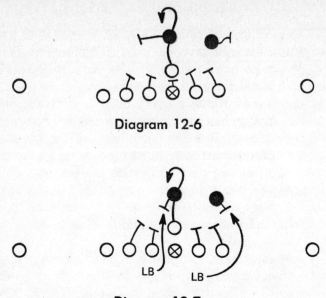

Diagram 12-6

Diagram 12-7

throw while moving one way but not the other, it may be wise to bring pressure on him from his strong side.

From scouting reports and game films, determine the opponent's passer protection system. Are they using a zone cup protection or man-for-man assignments on their drop-back action? Remaining backs generally pick up rushers on the outside of the cup in a zone defense (Diagram 12-6). In man-for-man protection a back is usually assigned to the inside linebacker or his side if he shoots (Diagram 12-7).

Many teams use both systems alternating them to confuse the defense.

From this analysis determine your best method of attack. Where and how can you attain a successful overload? What types of stunts can you use without seriously affecting the under-coverage from your linebackers? Determine what new techniques, if any, may be required of individuals in your rushing unit. Identify what techniques will be most appropriate to emphasize during the week of practice. Study the individual offensive blockers for weaknesses.

In practice, set up the various offensive passing sets and walk the rushing unit through their assignments. Be sure that in each maneuver responsibility is designated for the draw play center screens, and outside leverage.

DEVELOPING THE DELAY PLAN

Again using the scout reports, determine the one or two favorite or most dangerous receivers. It is advisable to confine your delay tactics to no more than two receivers on a given play. Remember that the defensive men assigned to this task will be delayed themselves in carrying out other responsibilities.

The delay techniques to be utilized will be determined by the favorite routes of these favorite receivers. The defender's position on the receiver must afford him the opportunity to effectively delay or cut off those patterns. In turn, these positions must be consistent with the overall defensive alignment, considering also the defender's responsibility in the running defense.

One cannot effectively delay, rush, and defend the pass zones all at the same time. You must develop separate plans for each strategy, or at best, plans that emphasize only two of the three strategies on any given play.

DEVELOPING THE GAME PLAN

The defensive coordinator should have the responsibility for developing the defensive game plan and all other members of the defensive staff make their contributions. The staff member assigned the primary responsibility for pass defense should develop this phase of the defensive game plan.

The defensive plan is based on evaluation of the opponent's strengths and weaknesses compared to those of your own team. In addition, assumptions must be made as to how the opponent will most likely play the game against your team, his probable game plan.

Based on all available information a general strategy must be established. Will your team play a conservative defensive game and wait for the breaks or will you gamble, penetrate, stunt, and maintain a strong pressure on the opponent's offense? Naturally, your objective is to win the game, but how do you intend to do it?

A decision must be made as to which of your defensive formations will be emphasized in this game. What line and linebacker adjustments can you make against their various offensive sets to strengthen each defense? What adjustments in your secondary will assure the best support against the run and the strongest coverage when pass is indicated?

Based upon the opponent's tendencies a plan must be devised for the use of your defenses. I have found it helpful to draw the opponent's favorite offensive sets on large cards, then list the defenses, adjustments, and stunts that should work best against each set on the back of each card. These cards can be used during the week in training the defensive signal caller and kept available for reference on the practice field and during the game.

Finally, designations must be given to each new adjustment and stunt that has been devised for this opponent and this game. These designations need to be incorporated into the system that you use to communicate with your defensive quarterback during the game. If a number of new terms or signals are being added, it is wise to start using them in practice sessions early in the week so that everyone will be thoroughly familiar with them by game time.

DEVELOPING THE PRACTICE PLANS

All of the analysis and decision-making referred to above must be accomplished by the defensive staff during the weekend. These tasks must be completed before work can begin on the development of a productive set of daily practice plans for the week. Too frequently, I have seen football staffs that failed to do their homework prior to Monday. They go into the Monday practice half prepared, indecisive about their defensive plans and strategy, and consequently waste a practice period. It is even worse to introduce adjustments and techniques to the squad on Monday when their soundness has not been established by careful deliberation and staff discussion, then to change these adjustments on Tuesday or Wednesday when it becomes obvious that they are not advisable. This type of coaching confuses the players and breeds a lack of confidence in the coaching staff and the game preparation.

A typical week of mid-season defensive practice could follow the format outlined below:

Monday

Varsity in sweat clothes. A heavy emphasis on running and the kicking game. An offensive unit will present the opponent's favorite formations and run the favorite running plays from each formation. The defensive players line up in our choice of defensive alignments for each formation and merely observe. We will show the blocking at the hole on any key play and the defensive stunts we are going to call to put our personnel in the best position against this type of blocking.

Next we separate the defensive backs and linebackers and they take their positions while a skeleton offensive unit runs through their favorite pass patterns from each formation. Again the defense is moved into the adjustments we have determined for each set and merely observes.

Our major coaching objective on Monday is to introduce on the field the opponent's offensive sets and their favorite plays and to acquaint our team with the defensive alignments we intend to make. On this date we are more concerned with individual positions in the adjustments than we are with technique.

Tuesday

Practice begins with a review of basic individual defensive skills and any new individual techniques that may be required in this game.

The mid-practice period is devoted to unit work. Linebackers will alternate working with the line on run defense and the backs on pass defense.

The defensive team will work as a whole during the last portion of practice. An offensive unit will run the opponent's sets, plays, and pattern as we move the ball to various field positions to simulate game conditions. Our defensive quarterback will call appropriate adjustments, stunts, and coverages as we react in full speed dummy scrimmage conditions.

Wednesday

Our work Wednesday is essentially the same as Tuesday except that we pick up pace, doing considerable live contact work in all phases of the practice to get the timing and the rhythm of our defensive play. Detailed individual corrections are being made as well as any slight modifications of the defensive plans that may seem advisable.

The latter portion of full team practice will be devoted to goal line defense at both our end of the field and our opponent's.

Thursday

We devote the bulk of our time again to individual and unit work. The defensive backfield and linebackers spend considerable time working as a unit against a skeleton pass offense, reviewing coverages against all favorite sets and patterns. This work is done full speed live, but with no tackling.

The full team portion of practice is largely devoted to a game-conditions, dummy scrimmage with no live tackling. We will move the ball up and down the field reviewing every possible defensive situation. In this period we are providing a last full speed rehearsal to be certain that all players are correctly recognizing the offensive sets, taking their positions accordingly, and performing their technique as we have coached them during the week. Our defensive signal caller receives training in calling our defenses based upon field position and the tendencies which have been outlined for him.

Friday

Our last practice is quick and short. We run through an abbreviated pre-game warm-up, review aspects of our kicking game, then break into offensive and defensive groups.

We set up a skeleton offensive group in one of the opponent's formations and then have our defense line up in our basic formation. A coach calls out a stunt or coverage and on the snap all move to their responsibilities. We will do this from all of our defensive formations against each of their favorite sets. To save time in this drill we have all defensive personnel on the field at one time. We line them up in position by substitution order and have them move together on the snap. If we had three orders of substitution they would line up in our basic 52 defense as illustrated in Diagram 12-8. Besides serving as a quick defensive review, any player who misses an assignment is readily identified. We can also conveniently quiz all personnel of a particular position as to what their responsibility is, how they move on the snap, what their reaction is to a run, and what reaction they will make if a pass develops.

The laws of learning indicate that a person will learn a new skill or concept more efficiently if it is presented to him briefly over several periods rather than in one large dose. A week of practice

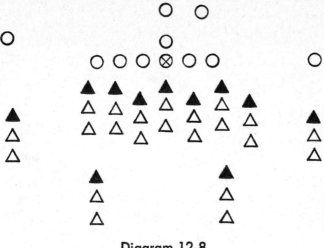

Diagram 12-8

should be developed on this premise. New material should be introduced early in the week then reviewed and expanded during each day of practice.

The whole plan of defense for the next game—the "big picture"—should be presented to the team on Monday. This plan should then be broken into units of instruction for each position and for each segment or unit of the defense. Next, a logical day-by-day sequence of presentation for these instructional units should be laid out, culminating in a final full team review on the day before the game.

INDEX